From Your Friends At **The MAILBOX®** Magazine

MAY

A MONTH OF IDEAS AT YOUR FINGERTIPS!

PRESCHOOL– KINDERGARTEN

W9-ARU-051

WRITTEN BY

Barbara Backer, Jan Brennan, Linda Gordetsky,
Ada Hanley Goren, Lucia Kemp Henry, Susan M. Hohbach,
Marie Iannetti, Angie Kutzer, Carrie Lacher, Linda Ludlow,
Suzanne Moore, Sharon Murphy, Vicki Pacchetti, Mackie Rhodes

EDITED BY

Lynn Bemer Coble, Ada Hanley Goren, Laurel Robinson,
Jennifer Rudisill, Gina Sutphin

ILLUSTRATED BY

Jennifer T. Bennett, Cathy Spangler Bruce,
Pam Crane, Clevell Harris,
Lucia Kemp Henry, Susan Hodnett,
Sheila Krill, Rob Mayworth,
Rebecca Saunders, Barry Slate

TYPESET BY

Lynette Maxwell

COVER DESIGNED BY

Jennifer T. Bennett

TABLE OF CONTENTS

May Calendar

National Strawberry Month

Celebrate the strawberry with a "berry" special day at school. Display a basket of washed strawberries and allow each child to take one for observation. Encourage students to taste their berries, then use all five senses to describe the berries in a class discussion. Extend the theme with activities from pages 76–85. What a splendid, special, strawberry day!

National Physical Fitness And Sports Month

If warmer weather has your youngsters yearning for a day in the sun, plan a fitness day for outdoor fun. Lead your children in a march around the school grounds, some toe touches in the sunshine, a few knee bends on the playground, then a stretch-out on the grass. For more information about promoting physical activity, write to the President's Council On Physical Fitness And Sports, 701 Pennsylvania Avenue NW, Suite 250, Washington, DC 20004.

National Egg Month

The month of May pays tribute to the versatility and good nutrition of the egg. Most students will associate eggs with breakfast foods, so do some cooking in your classroom to show that eggs can be found in cookies, brownies, and even meat loaf! Save the eggshells for an art project in which your students create a mosaic with pieces of the shells. Your youngsters will know eggs inside and out!

National Family Month™

This monthlong national commemoration is celebrated each year from Mother's Day through Father's Day to promote strong, supportive family bonds. Reinforce the importance of families by having students share special family customs with classmates. Invite parents and family members to a special family time at school. Ask each parent to share with your students something that is meaningful to their family, such as a storybook, a favorite cookie recipe, a song, or a scrapbook. After the sharing time, have each parent write a sentence or two telling why families are important. Have each student illustrate the page written by her parent. Compile the pages into a take-home book that families can read together.

Be Kind To Animals Week®
(First Full Week Of May)

Sponsored by the American Humane Association, this week is dedicated to promoting kindness to and care of our pets. Discuss how pets are dependent on their owners for food, shelter, and love. Share a story about special pet care by reading *Michael And The Cats* by Darbara Abercrombie (Margaret K. McElderry Books) or *Can I Keep Him?* by Steven Kellogg (Puffin Books). Then have children name different kinds of pets. Record their responses on chart paper; then create a class big book as children list ways to take care of each kind of pet.

Adele

You have to walk a dog.

3

National Transportation Week
(Week Including The Third Friday In May)

Focus on things that take us from *here* to *there* during National Transportation Week. Introduce various forms of transportation to your students with *The Big Book Of Things That Go* (Dorling Kindersley). Then sing a tribute to the many forms of transportation with Wee Sing *Wheels, Sounds, And Songs* (Price, Stern, and Sloan).

1—May Day

May Day means that spring is in full swing! Take your class on a walk to observe springtime happenings, from birds building nests to flowers in bloom. Back in the classroom, have students color and cut out construction-paper flowers to fill individual May baskets (plastic strawberry crates with pipe-cleaner handles). Encourage your youngsters to distribute the baskets to special people at home or school with the hearty greeting, "Happy May Day!"

1—Mother Goose Day

Invite Peter, Peter Pumpkin Eater; Little Jack Horner; and Jack Sprat into your classroom for Mother Goose Day! Your students will enjoy the pictures in *Tomie dePaola's Mother Goose*, illustrated by Tomie dePaola (G. P. Putman's Sons) or *Mother Goose*, illustrated by Tasha Tudor (Random House Books For Young Readers). After sharing these Mother Goose books with your class, encourage students to recite their favorite nursery rhymes.

5—Cinco De Mayo

This Mexican national holiday commemorates the anniversary of a victorious military battle on May 5, 1862. The holiday is observed with parades, festivals, dances, and speeches. Create a *fiesta* in your classroom with a Mexican Hat Dance around a *sombrero,* and some *pan dulces* (sweet pastries) to munch afterward. Then introduce some of Mexico's culture by reading *Count Your Way Through Mexico* by Jim Haskins (Carolrhoda Books, Inc.).

Mother's Day (Second Sunday In May)

Mother's Day was first observed in 1907 at the request of Anna Jarvis, who wished to recognize all mothers on the anniversary of her own mother's death. Today we honor our mothers with cards, flowers, and gifts in appreciation for the many things they do for us. The ideas and activities found on pages 26–29 are guaranteed to bring Mother's Day smiles and plenty of hugs and kisses!

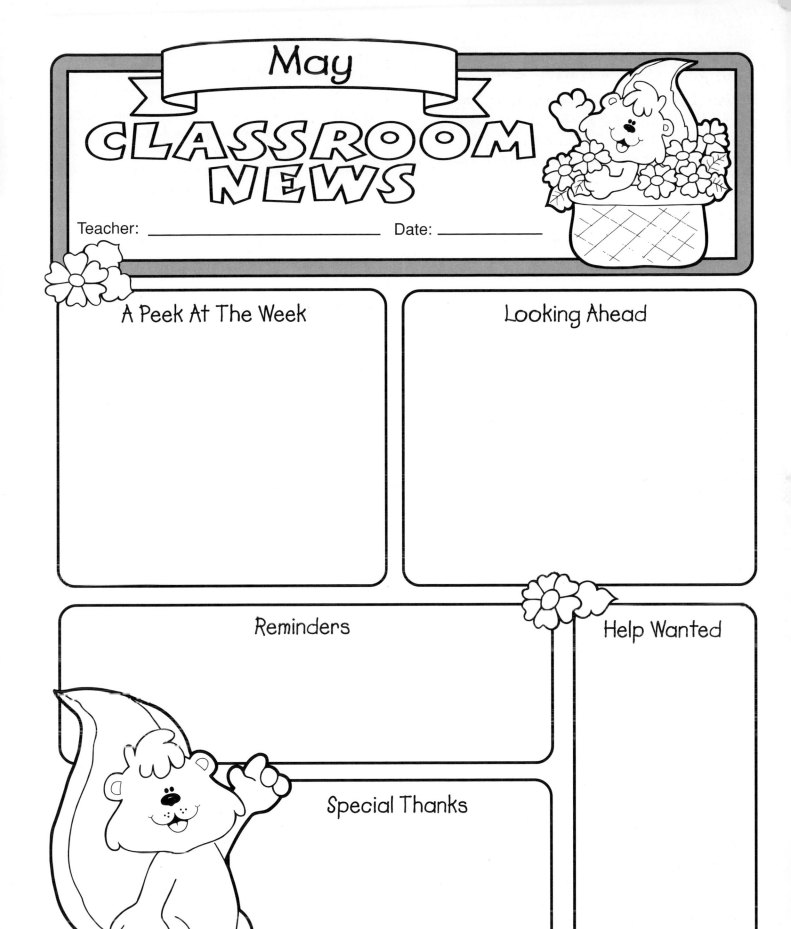

May

CLASSROOM NEWS

Teacher: _____   Date: _____

A Peek At The Week

Looking Ahead

Reminders

Help Wanted

Special Thanks

From Caterpillar To Butterfly

Use the activities below to help your little ones explore the mysterious metamorphosis of this interesting insect.

ideas contributed by Suzanne Moore and Angie Kutzer

Baby Butterflies

Begin this unit by discussing animal babies and their parents. Name an animal and ask a student volunteer to name its offspring. For example, say, "A cat has…" and your youngsters will respond, "kittens." End the discussion with, "A butterfly has…." After explaining that not all babies resemble their parents, read the story *Butterfly* by Mary Ling (Dorling Kindersley, Inc.) Your youngsters will be excited to learn that caterpillars are really baby butterflies!

Finger Flutters

This fingerplay will transform little fingers into caterpillars and butterflies!

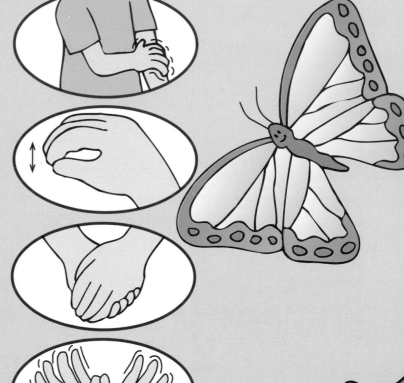

Here comes a caterpillar,
Creeping up a tree.

It's munching every leaf in sight,
Hungry as can be.

It sheds its skin and forms a shell;
The changes we can't see.

Then out of the shell a butterfly comes,
Flying fancy-free!

Creepy Crawlers

Your little ones will have fun creating their own creepy-crawly caterpillars in this activity. Show your youngsters some photos of caterpillars from nonfiction books. Explain that a caterpillar's body is made up of 13 segments, plus a head. Can they count the segments of each caterpillar in the photos?

Then invite your students to make their own caterpillars. To prepare, cut sheets of large-bubbled packing wrap into strips—each strip 14 bubbles long. For each child, tape a strip to a table or washable tray. Have each child brush a bubble strip with tempera paint. Then have him place a 6" x 18" piece of construction paper over the bubble strip and rub gently. Ask him to lift the paper off the bubbles and count the segments of his painted caterpillar. When the paint is dry, encourage each child to use markers and wiggle eyes to complete his creepy-crawly critter. Let the finished caterpillars creep onto a bulletin board for a colorful display.

Caterpillar Concentration

Add a twist to the traditional game of Concentration by using this caterpillar theme. Cut circles from green tagboard or collect green, disposable plates. Draw a face on one of the circles. Tape the tops of the circles to your chalkboard to resemble a caterpillar. Program the space behind each circle with a letter, a shape, a numeral, or a sight word you'd like your students to identify. Make sure each symbol is represented twice.

To play, invite a child to lift a segment of the caterpillar; then encourage another student volunteer to try to find the matching symbol by lifting another segment. If the symbols match, the segments are removed. Continue until all the matches have been found. Vary the game by programming other skills or by adding more segments.

Fancy Footwork

Get those little legs moving with some caterpillar locomotion! Take your children outside and divide them into groups of two or three. Instruct the children in each group to form a caterpillar by connecting hands-to-shoulders. Then encourage the caterpillars to travel to a designated spot and back without becoming disconnected. As the caterpillars become proficient in maneuvering all of those legs, have some groups combine to make longer caterpillars.

Watch And Wonder

The best way to understand the changes that occur with caterpillars and butterflies is to actually observe the process. Although caterpillars can be found in many areas, a few types are harmful. To be on the safe side, order a few larvae from Carolina Biological Supply Company at 1-800-334-5551. The larvae arrive in a vial with a food supply to last until the chrysalis stage. There are also instructions for setting up a butterfly habitat. Your little ones will be mesmerized by the experience. It's also a wonderful opportunity for journaling, so watch, wonder, and *write!*

Metamorphosis Movement

Share the story *Where Butterflies Grow* by Joanne Ryder (Puffin Unicorn Books) with your children. After the story, name and review the four stages of a butterfly's transformation—*egg, caterpillar, chrysalis,* and *butterfly.* Show the corresponding illustrations in the close-up boxes from the book. Invite your students to imitate the changing process as you read the story again. They will enjoy curling up inside their eggs, stretching out of their old skins, climbing up the stems, resting in their chrysalides, and flapping their wings!

From Egg To Butterfly

After your children have pantomimed the changes in "Metamorphosis Movement," provide the materials to make this life-cycle card. Each child will need a copy of page 12, a popcorn kernel, four small pom-poms, an uncooked rigatoni noodle, a 1 1/2-inch piece of pipe cleaner, glue, crayons, and glitter.

Have each child color and cut out a card pattern. Help him to crease the card pattern forward and backward on the dotted lines. Then help him fold his pattern horizontally and vertically on the dotted lines to make a card. To make the butterfly pop out, fold it forward and downward on the dotted lines across the butterfly's wings.

Instruct the child to glue the popcorn kernel (egg) onto the top leaf, the pom-poms (caterpillar) onto the bottom leaf, and the rigatoni (chrysalis) under the stem. Then have him insert the piece of pipe cleaner inside the chrysalis. When the glue is dry, have the child open the card and decorate the butterfly with glitter. Leave the card open until that glue is dry. Your little ones will flutter home in a hurry to show off their life-cycle knowledge using this card!

"Meta-munch-osis"

Your little ones will feel like hungry caterpillars as they munch, munch, munch on this fun snack. To prepare, cut a classroom supply of Fruit Roll-Ups® diagonally, making two triangles. Each child will need two coffee-stirring sticks and two fruit-snack triangles. You will also need to provide the class with a bag of large marshmallows and a bag of small marshmallows (pastel colored if desired).

Encourage each youngster to push one large marshmallow onto the end of one of her stirring sticks and slide small marshmallows onto the rest of the stirring stick to make a caterpillar. Have her transform the caterpillar into a butterfly by sticking the second stirring stick through a marshmallow in the middle of the caterpillar and threading on the fruit-snack triangles (wings) as shown. Don't be surprised if these butterflies take flight before they are gobbled up!

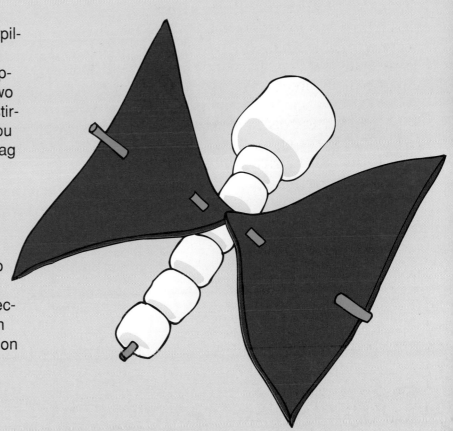

Creations From Explorations

Manipulatives are great tools for sparking the imagination. During free-exploration time, encourage children to create caterpillars and butterflies from manipulatives such as pattern blocks, attribute blocks, and other building sets. Take an instant photo of each child's creation; then attach the picture to chart paper and write his dictation about his project.

Soon You'll Be A Butterfly!

Butterfly egg on the leaf of a tree,
You're just as tiny as you can be.

Out comes caterpillar; you must eat.
The leaf you're on is quite a treat!

Caterpillar starts to grow and grow.
Shed your skin and what do you know?

Caterpillar, take just one more bite.
Now it's time to say, "Good night!"

Chrysalis on a branch up high,
Soon you'll be a butterfly!

Butterflies And Me

Kindle your students' critical-thinking skills with this comparison booklet. In advance duplicate pages 13–15 for each child. Provide a 7 1/2" x 5" piece of tagboard for each child. Have each student cut out the last page of his booklet and glue it to the tagboard. Instruct each student to cut out the rest of his pages on the dotted lines. Stack the butterfly pages in order and staple them to the left side of the tagboard page. Stack the child pages in order and staple them to the right side of the tagboard page. You will also need an individual picture of each student, a class supply of small wiggle eyes, a class supply of tongue shapes cut from red felt, several colored ink pads, and paper towels.

Have your little ones brainstorm a list of ways in which they are different from butterflies. Then help them to complete the booklet using the following directions:

Booklet Cover: Color the butterfly and write your name. Glue a photo of yourself to the page.

Page 1: Color the butterfly and draw its six legs. Draw a full-body portrait of yourself.

Page 2: Color the butterfly and glue a wiggle eye to its face. Glue a tongue shape to the page.

Page 3: Use thumbprints to decorate the butterfly's wings. Draw two antennae on the butterfly. Draw your nose.

Page 4: Draw several butterflies. Illustrate a movement of your choice and write it in the blank.

Page 5: Color the picture; then glue a square piece of a paper towel to the bed to make a blanket.

Tongue-Tied

This quiet game can reinforce a skill of your choice while extending the butterfly theme. To prepare, make several construction-paper flower cutouts and program each one with a letter of the alphabet. Tape these cutouts to a wall within children's reach.

A butterfly sips nectar through its tongue, which is shaped like a long tube. Its tongue rolls up when not in use. Give each of your young butterflies a party blower and let her practice straightening and curling this imitation butterfly tongue. Direct the children's attention to the flower cutouts. Review each letter's name and the sound it makes. To play the game, call out the name of a food that begins with one of the designated letters. Invite a student volunteer to "fly" to the cutouts and "drink" from the correct flower. Continue until interest wanes or until butterfly bellies are full!

Delicate Wings

Unique butterflies will be gliding through your classroom when your little nature lovers finish this activity. Using several different colors of tissue paper, make a butterfly for each child by folding a piece of colored tissue paper and cutting a wing shape as shown. Staple the wings together approximately one inch from the fold as shown. Carefully slide a tongue depressor through the paper and twist it so that the staples are in the middle of a flat side of the stick. Crease the wings apart at the staples. Have each child use the tissue-paper scraps to create colorful designs on the wings of his butterfly. To make the butterfly flap its wings, instruct the child to hold the end of the stick and gently move it up and down. Play some light, bouncy "butterfly music" and invite children to fly their butterflies around the room. What a beautiful sight!

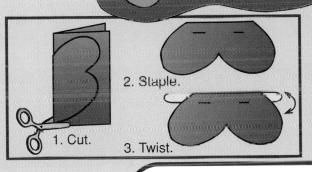

1. Cut.
2. Staple.
3. Twist.

Butterfly Books

The Lamb And The Butterfly
Written by Arnold Sundgaard
Published by Scholastic Inc.

Look...A Butterfly
Written by David Cutts
Published by Troll Associates

The Caterpillar And The Polliwog
Written by Jack Kent
Published by Simon & Schuster
  Books For Young Readers

Amazing Butterflies & Moths
Written by John Still
Published by Alfred A. Knopf, Inc.

The Great Monarch Butterfly Chase
Written by R. W. N. Prior
Published by Bradbury Press

A Butterfly Is Born
Written by Melvin Berger
Published by Newbridge
  Communications, Inc.

Pop-Up Card

Use with "From Egg To Butterfly" on page 8.

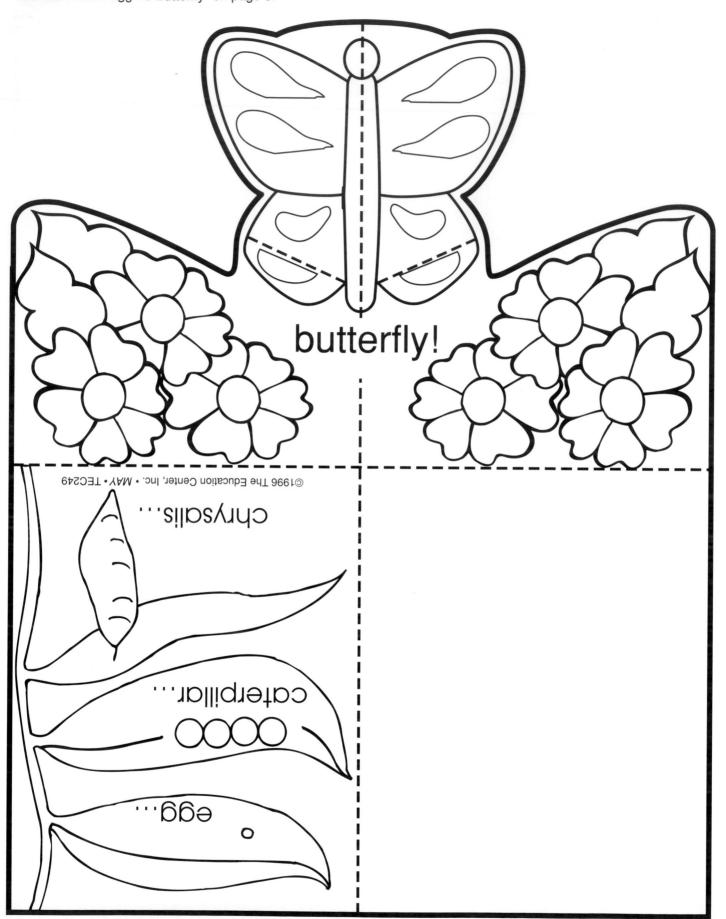

butterfly!

©1996 The Education Center, Inc. • *MAY* • TEC249

chrysalis...

caterpillar...

egg...

Butterflies

And Me

by_____

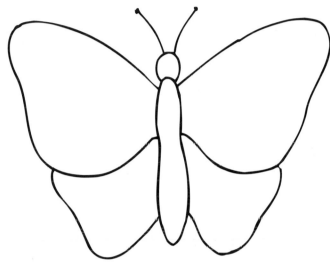

Butterflies have six legs.

1

I have two legs.

1

Booklet Pages
Use with "Butterflies And Me" on page 10.

Butterflies taste with their feet.

2

2 I taste with my tongue.

Butterflies smell with their antennae.

3

3 I smell with my nose.

Butterflies fly.

4

4 I can _____.

Butterflies sleep at night
and so do I.
Good night!

FLOWER POWER

A BOUQUET OF BLOOMING IDEAS

Plant a garden of delights in your classroom with this flower-filled unit. Excite budding minds with this bouquet of springtime-fresh ideas; then watch bright eyes and happy smiles blossom on your little ones!

ideas contributed by Carrie Lacher and Sharon Murphy

FLOWER FACTS

Dig right into your flower study by bringing in a bouquet of fresh, inexpensive flowers. Include several different varieties. Invite youngsters to examine the flowers up close, using their senses of sight, touch, and smell. Encourage students to comment on the similarities and differences among the flowers.

After the flower exploration, ask students to contribute their knowledge to a chart titled "Flower Facts." Besides their hands-on experience, youngsters may want to tell about people they know who like flowers, or where flowers are found. After everyone has had a chance to contribute, have your students draw flowers in the margins of the chart paper. Display the chart on a classroom wall throughout your study.

Flower Facts
My mom likes flowers.
Jeffrey
We have yellow flowers in our yard.
Miguel
Some flowers are on trees.
Elizabeth

PAINT A RAINBOW

Flowers come in a variety of beautiful colors. Introduce your little ones to some of the many colors of flowers with the book *Planting A Rainbow* by Lois Ehlert (Harcourt Brace Jovanovich). In this story a mother and child plant flowers in a garden. They watch as bulbs, seeds, and plants grow into a rainbow of colorful blooms.

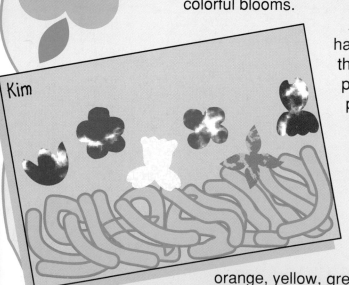

Kim

After sharing the text and vivid illustrations of the book, have each student create a rainbow—by painting, rather than planting! In advance add dish detergent to shallow pans of green, red, orange, yellow, purple, and blue tempera paint. Cut sponges into several different flower shapes. Provide each child with a 12" x 18" sheet of light blue construction paper. Have each child use the green paint to finger-paint the bottom of his sheet of paper to make grass. Next have students take turns dipping the flower-shaped sponges into the pans of paint and pressing them onto their paper. Ask more advanced students to sponge-paint the flowers in the order of the colors in a rainbow—red, orange, yellow, green, blue, and purple. After the paint dries, mount the rainbows on a bulletin board titled "Painting A Rainbow."

FLOWERPOT GIFTS

Even a child knows that flowers make wonderful gifts! Read the book *Flower Garden* by Eve Bunting (Harcourt Brace & Company) for a story of a garden gift; then invite each of your students to plant a flower as a gift for a school helper. If there are more helpers in your school than students in your class, be sure to plant extra flowers.

Provide each child with a miniature clay flowerpot and a variety of art supplies— such as paint pens and stickers—for decorating her flowerpot. After she finishes decorating, spray the pot with clear acrylic and allow it to dry. Then have each child fill her pot with potting soil and add a few fast-growing seeds, such as marigolds. Place the flowerpots in a sunny spot in your classroom. Assist students in nurturing their plants with the appropriate amount of water. Encourage your youngsters to examine their flowerpots daily to check for signs of growth.

Once the marigolds have bloomed, complete the project by making a gift tag as shown; then duplicate one for each student. Help each youngster write the name of a school helper on her gift tag; then have her sign her own name. Next have each child color and cut out her gift tag. Use tape to attach each student's gift tag to her flowerpot. Set the pots aside for students to distribute in "A Parade Of Petals" on page 19.

PETAL PAGES

Encourage youngsters to explore their creativity with their own unique flower books. For each child, duplicate the flower pattern on page 20 and trim the labels off the bottom. Glue the flower pattern to the front of a folded sheet of 18" x 24" construction paper. Add four sheets of white paper to the inside of the book; then staple along the fold. Print "[child's name]'s Flower Book" on the front cover.

Have each child use crayons or markers to decorate the front cover of her book. Next have students search for pictures of flowers in garden magazines and catalogs. Ask each child to cut out four pictures and glue one picture to each page in her book. Below each picture write the child's dictation describing the flower. Have the children share their finished books with classmates.

FLOWER ARRANGEMENTS

Sorting skills will be blossoming with this activity! To prepare, purchase silk roses, daisies, and tulips from a local craft store. Remove the blossoms from their stems. Place the blossoms in a basket or flowerpot. Next cut a picture of each of the three flowers from a garden magazine or catalog. Label each picture and attach it to a smaller flowerpot or basket.

Show your children photos of roses, daisies, and tulips. Place the labeled containers and the basket of blooms in the middle of your group. Help your students sort the flowers into the correct containers. To keep their classification skills growing, have your students sort the blooms by color, too.

FLANNELBOARD FLOWERS

Have some flannelboard fun with this rhyme that teaches the three basic parts of a flower: *stem, petals,* and *leaves.* Duplicate and color the flower and bee patterns on page 20. Laminate the designs before cutting out each one. Attach the hook side of a piece of self-adhesive Velcro® to the back of each cutout.

My flower grows up toward the sky,
Leaves and stem and petals high.

Place the flower on the flannelboard.

See the green leaves near the ground—
On the stem is where they're found.

Point to the leaves.
Point to the stem.

See the petals, count with me.
How many petals do you see?
1, 2, 3, 4, 5, 6, 7, 8, 9, 10

Point to each petal and count;

See the honeybee come callin',
Buzzin' 'round in search of pollen.

Place the honeybee on the flannelboard.

My flower smiles and says, "Hello."
The bee says, "Thanks!" before he goes.

Remove the honeybee from the flannelboard.

THE PARTS OF THE FLOWER

Provide youngsters the opportunity to demonstrate their understanding of the three main parts of a flower by having them label their own flower pictures. Duplicate the patterns on page 20 for each student. Have each child color his flower and then cut out the flower-part labels at the bottom of the sheet. Provide help as each child glues a label to each flower part on his paper. Display the completed flower models for a garden of colorful knowledge sure to brighten your classroom!

A FLAVORFUL FLOWER

After making and eating these edible flowers, youngsters will have an even better knowledge of a flower's parts.

Ingredients For One:
2 vanilla wafers
1 spoonful peanut butter
8 miniature chocolate chips
10 pieces candy corn
1/2 celery stalk
vanilla icing, tinted with green
food coloring

Use a plastic knife to spread peanut butter on one vanilla wafer. Put a few miniature chocolate chips atop the peanut butter. Place the tips of the candy-corn pieces around the edge of the wafer to resemble petals. Place the celery stalk at the bottom of the flower to represent the flower's stem. Cut the other vanilla wafer in half. Spread the green icing on each half of the wafer. Place the wafer halves on opposite sides at the bottom of the stalk to represent leaves.

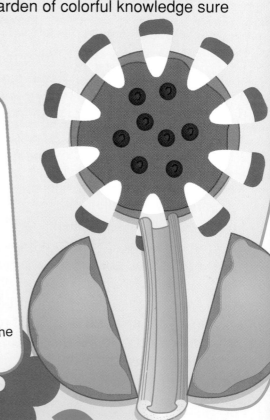

LAVENDER-FLOWER PLAY DOUGH

Fill your classroom with the wonderful aroma of lavender with this new variety of play dough.

Ingredients:
3 cups flour
2 cups water
3/4 cup salt
3 tablespoons oil

3 tablespoons cream of tartar
1/8 cup violet powdered tempera paint
10–20 drops lavender-flower essential oil
purple glitter

In a large pot, mix together the first five ingredients until smooth. Place the pot over medium heat, stirring constantly until the mixture forms into a large ball. While the mixture is still warm, place it on a floured cutting board and knead in additional flour until the dough has a silky texture. Add powdered paint and lavender essential oil and knead thoroughly. Sprinkle with purple glitter and knead again. Store in an airtight container.

Once the play dough is ready, give each child a small amount on a sheet of waxed paper. Invite him to mold the play dough or to flatten it and use small, flower-shaped cookie cutters to cut "scent-sational" flower shapes from it!

COUNTING ON FLOWERS

For counting practice with a flower theme, read the book *Counting Wildflowers* by Bruce McMillan (William Morrow & Company, Inc.). After sharing this colorful counting book with your students, have them use flower shapes and a flower wand to practice counting numerals. In advance, die-cut ten flower shapes from different colors of construction paper (or cut them by hand). Label each flower with a different numeral from "one" to "ten". Obtain a length of 1/4-inch dowel and hot-glue one or two fabric blossoms to one end of it. Next cut two lengths of 1/4-inch green fabric ribbon and hot-glue the ribbon lengths to the flower end of the wand. Invite each child, in turn, to use the flower wand to point to the numbered flowers as she counts them.

A PARADE OF PETALS

Conclude your flower theme with a springtime flower parade. In advance, purchase several pieces of fabric with flowery patterns. Create capes or skirts by cutting the pieces of fabric into large squares and rectangles. For each piece of fabric, attach the hook side of a piece of self-adhesive Velcro® to one corner and the loop side to the other corner as shown. To create flower hats, hot-glue fabric blossoms to several dress-up hats.

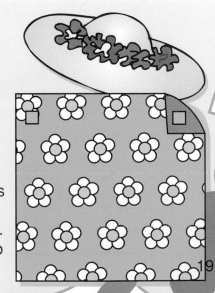

On the day of this activity, invite each child to put on either a decorated hat, cape, or skirt. Provide each child with his flowerpot gift for his chosen school helper. (See "Flowerpot Gifts" on page 17.) Now grab your flower wand and lead your parade of little ones around the school. Delight in the surprised looks of school helpers as your parade stops to deliver flowerpots of thanks!

Patterns

Use the flower and bee patterns with "Petal Pages" on page 17 and "Flannelboard Flowers" on page 18.
Use all the patterns with "The Parts Of The Flower" on page 18.

| Petals | Stem | Leaves |

PICNIC PLEASURES

Quick, pack the picnic basket! May is the perfect time for a picnic—spring breezes, blossoming flowers, and antsy children. This fun theme unit is packed full of picnic-perfect ideas that span the curriculum!

ideas contributed by Jan Brennan and Sharon Murphy

Picnic Pals

Try this twist on a teddy bears' picnic to begin your picnic theme. In advance, spread a tablecloth or blanket on the floor. Place two teddy bears and a picnic basket in the middle of the picnic cloth. Fill the picnic basket with pairs of picnic items (such as two paper plates, two spoons, and two napkins) and doubles of picnic-type plastic food (such as two apples, two sandwiches, and two empty boxes of animal crackers). Provide enough food or picnic items so that each child has one item. If you have an odd number of students, add a picnic item for yourself.

Invite your little ones to gather in a circle around the picnic cloth. Pass the picnic basket around the circle and have each child remove one item from the basket. When everyone has a picnic item, ask each child to find the classmate with the matching item. This person will be his Picnic Pal.

Once everyone has found his Picnic Pal, explain to your children that the teddy bears are also Picnic Pals and that they need help in setting up their picnic. Ask your students which of the picnic items the bears will need first. Have the two students holding those items place them in front of the bears. Continue until all the picnic items are on the cloth. Then tell students that this activity was practice for an upcoming event—a real picnic! (See the activities on pages 22–23.) Place the picnic items, cloth, and bears in the dramatic-play area for your youngsters to enjoy throughout your picnic unit.

Favorite Picnic Foods

Your little ones are sure to like picnics, but chances are they will all have different picnic-food favorites. Find out what your youngsters like to eat at picnics when they create this class book.

Provide each child with a paper plate. Ask her to draw a picture of her favorite picnic food on her plate. (Or have each child cut a picture of her favorite picnic food from a magazine and glue it on her plate.) Then print "[Child's name] likes [picnic food]" below her picture. To make the front cover for the book, write "Good Food For A Picnic" on a paper plate. Stack the finished plates under the front cover and bind the book along the left edge. Place the completed book in the reading center and invite picnic pals to read the book together.

Jamie likes
fried chicken.

Paper-Bag Picnic Baskets

Youngsters will delight in making their very own picnic baskets. Prepare a tray of brown tempera paint and several 1 1/2-inch square sponges. Give each child a brown paper lunch bag and ask him to write his name on the bottom of the bag. Encourage each child to sponge-paint the front of his bag to resemble a woven picnic basket as shown. Allow the paint to dry thoroughly; then turn the bag to the other side and repeat the process. When that paint has dried, staple a 2" x 12" strip of construction paper to the bag to create a handle. Set these miniature picnic baskets aside to use with "Picnic Preparations."

A-Tisket, A-Tasket, Fill The Picnic Basket!

When you are ready for little ones to pack their picnic lunches, teach them this delightful melody.

My Picnic Basket
(sung to the tune of "A Tisket, A Tasket")

A tisket, a tasket,
a special picnic basket.
I made it strong; it won't be long,
'Til I begin to pack it.

To pack it, to pack it,
I cannot wait to pack it.
Crackers, fruit, and sandwich, please,
To put inside my basket.

My basket, my basket,
My special picnic basket.
I'll fill it up with such good food!
I'm glad I made my basket.

Picnic Preparations

You're sure to get an enthusiastic response when you invite your little ones to pack their own lunches for a class picnic. Provide crackers, a variety of fresh fruit, and the ingredients to make peanut-butter-and-jelly sandwiches. Invite each child to make his sandwich, pick a fruit, and count a specified number of crackers into a zippered plastic bag. Have him place all his picnic goodies and a napkin in his previously made picnic basket. Pack paper plates and paper cups in the real picnic basket, and take a drink cooler of lemonade or juice. Now you and your youngsters are all packed for a perfectly pleasing picnic. Mmmm, good!

Ready To Picnic?

Now that the picnic preparations are complete, you and your youngsters are ready to picnic! Teach youngsters this song as you travel to the perfect picnic spot.

Here We Go On A Picnic Today
(sung to the tune of "Here We Go 'Round The Mulberry Bush")

Here we go on a picnic today,
A picnic today, a picnic today.
Here we go on a picnic today,
On such a beautiful [day of the week].

This is the way we spread our cloth,
Spread our cloth, spread our cloth.
This is the way we spread our cloth,
On such a beautiful [day of the week].

Continue the song with additional verses:
This is the way we eat our lunch...
This is the way we play our games...
This is the way we clean it up...

After a delightful picnic, invite students to add a final verse to the picnic song on the walk back to their classroom.

We had fun on a picnic today,
A picnic today, a picnic today.
We had fun on a picnic today,
On such a beautiful [day of the week].

Picnic Games

The food might be gone, but the picnic is not over! Invite your little ones to join you in the picnic versions of these popular children's games.

• Play this picnic version of Telephone to sharpen your youngsters' listening skills. Ask your students to sit in a circle. To begin the game, whisper a picnic word, such as "watermelon," to one of your students. Then have that child whisper the same picnic word into his neighbor's ear. Have students continue in this manner until each child has had a turn. Ask the child who receives the word last to say the word aloud. Is it the same word that you started with? If so, you have a picnic full of good listeners!

• For this fun-filled memory game, you will need enough plastic picnic food and picnic items for each child and a real picnic basket. Have students gather in a circle and place the picnic basket and items in the middle. Begin by saying, "I'm going on a picnic and I'm taking a [picnic item]." Place that picnic item in the picnic basket. Then invite a student to repeat your sentence and add another picnic item. Continue until each child has had a turn. Encourage students to peek into the picnic basket to help them remember the previous items.

• Encourage your little ones to practice their gross-motor skills with this picnic jump-rope rhyme. Ask for a volunteer to help you turn the jump rope as students take turns jumping to this rhyme.

Out on a picnic, having so much fun,
There sat [child's name] out in the sun.

She ate and she ate and she ate her lunch,
How many sandwiches did she munch?

Count the number of jumps the child takes.

More Picnic Possibilities

Delight your little ones with these positively perfect ideas for extending your picnic theme!

Count On Ants

Picnics mean warm weather, tasty food—and ants! When students go to this picnic center, they can count on an army of ants to join them. To make this math center, program a set of white paper plates with different numerals from "one" to "ten". To make the plates look delicious, glue pictures of food cut from magazines onto each plate. Store the plates in a picnic basket. Purchase a supply of plastic ants from a local craft store or the Oriental Trading Company, Inc. (1-800-228-2269). Or, if desired, place ant stickers on pennies to use in this activity. Spread a picnic tablecloth over a table or on the floor in a center. Place the basket of plates and the ants on the tablecloth. To use this center, a youngster selects a plate from the basket and reads the numeral on the plate. After counting out the corresponding number of ants, he makes a trail of ants marching toward the plate.

Picnic Lotto

Test your youngsters' luck and matching skills with a picnic lotto game. Duplicate the lotto board on page 25 for yourself and each child. To make different boards for your students, cut the boards so that each one has only nine squares as shown. Next cut your board into the 16 squares to make the lotto cards. If desired, mount the cards on tagboard and laminate them for durability.

To play the game, distribute a gameboard and nine lotto markers to each student. Use the plastic ants from "Count On Ants" or raisins (to represent ants) for the markers, if desired. Display a lotto card for your students to see. If a child has a matching picture on his lotto board, he covers it with an ant or raisin. The game continues until a child covers three squares in a row—or, if desired, his whole card—and yells, "Picnic!" For an end-of-game treat, invite your little ones to sample chocolate-covered ants (chocolate-covered raisins)!

A Basket Of Books

Don't forget to pack these great books in your picnic basket! Take them along on your picnic or leave them at your reading center for some appetizing literature!

The Bears' Picnic
Written by Stan and Jan Berenstain
Published by Beginner Books

The Teddy Bears' Picnic
Written by Jimmy Kennedy
Published by Green Tiger Press

Once Upon A Picnic
Written by John Prater and Vivian French
Published by Candlewick Press

This Is The Bear And The Picnic Lunch
Written by Sarah Hayes
Published by Little, Brown and Company

It's The Bear!
Written by Jez Alborough
Published by Candlewick Press

The Mamas And The Papas

Encourage your little ones to show their appreciation and say, "Thank you," to their moms and dads—or to whomever their primary caregivers are—with these fun-filled activities. Plan a special unit on parents or—if your school calendar allows—use these activities separately on Mother's Day and Father's Day.

ideas contributed by Diane Gilliam, Marie Iannetti, and Linda Ludlow

Mommies And Daddies Are Special

Begin your unit by reading aloud the books *Mommies* and *Daddies* by Dian Curtis Regan (Scholastic Inc.). Both books depict the special relationships between parent and child and the special things they do together. After reading these stories, have each child share with his classmates one special thing he does with his mom and one special thing he does with his dad.

Mommy And Daddy Songs

Start your morning routine or circle time with these songs about moms and dads!

(both sung to the tune of "B-I-N-G-O")

I love her and she loves me,
And Mommy is her name-o.
M-O-M-M-Y
M-O-M-M-Y
M-O-M-M-Y
And Mommy is her name-o.

I love him and he loves me,
And Daddy is his name-o.
D-A-D-D-Y
D-A-D-D-Y
D-A-D-D-Y
And Daddy is his name-o.

(both sung to the tune of "Twinkle, Twinkle, Little Star")

Mommy, Mommy, let me say,
"I love you in every way.
I love you for all you do.
I love you for being you."
Mommy, Mommy, let me say,
"Have a Happy Mother's Day!"

Daddy, Daddy, let me say,
"I love you in every way.
I love you for all you do.
I love you for being you."
Daddy, Daddy, let me say,
"Have a Happy Father's Day!"

Getting To Know Mom And Dad

Help your youngsters get to know their caregivers better with this nifty idea. Either prior to your unit on parents or just before Mother's Day or Father's Day, duplicate and send home a copy of page 32 with each of your students. (Provide extra copies to children who wish to interview more than one parent.) Instruct each youngster to ask an older child or an adult to assist him in asking the questions, completing the form, and gluing on a picture of the parent interviewed. When a child returns his sheet to school, have him share what he learned about his parent with your class. Mount each child's sheet on a bulletin board or wall. Then give the display a three-dimensional effect by adding a twisted length of green bulletin-board paper and some green construction-paper leaves.

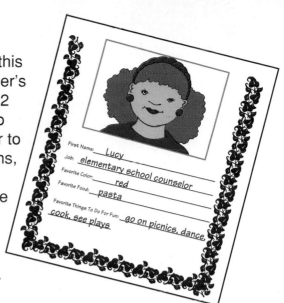

First Name: Lucy
Job: elementary school counselor
Favorite Color: red
Favorite Food: pasta
Favorite Things To Do For Fun: go on picnics, dance, cook, see plays

Mommy Books

Mothers Can Do Anything
Written by Joe Lasker
Published by Albert Whitman & Company

The Way Mothers Are
Written by Miriam Schlein
Published by Albert Whitman & Company

Mama, Do You Love Me?
Written by Barbara M. Joosse
Published by Scholastic Inc.

Love You Forever
Written by Robert Munsch
Published by Firefly Books Ltd.

The Mother's Day Mice
Written by Eve Bunting
Published by Scholastic Inc.

On Mother's Lap
Written by Ann Herbert Scott
Published by Scholastic Inc.

Mama Zooms
Written by Jane Cowen-Fletcher
Published by Scholastic Inc.

Daddy Books

Climbing Kansas Mountains
Written by George Shannon
Published by Bradbury Press

Can I Help?
Written by Marilyn Janovitz
Published by North-South Books Inc.

Guess How Much I Love You
Written by Sam McBratney
Published by Scholastic Inc.

Octopus Hug
Written by Laurence Pringle
Published by Boyds Mills Press, Inc.

My Father's Hands
Written by Joanne Ryder
Published by Morrow Junior Books

I Meant To Tell You
Written by James Stevenson
Published by Greenwillow Books

Today I'm Going Fishing With My Dad
Written by N. L. Sharp
Published by Boyds Mill Press, Inc.

All The Comforts Of Home

Provide your little ones with all the comforts of home when you transform your reading area into a warm and inviting environment. Place a rocker, a cushioned chair, or a small sofa in your reading area. Place a quilt or soft blanket on the chair or sofa. Position a small table next to the chair or sofa, and add a lamp for some soft light. Stock this center with books from these lists; then invite your students to visit this cozy center to enjoy some stories about moms and dads.

Marvelous Moms

Honor moms with these cute cards, gorgeous gifts, crafty corsages, and a special celebration!

"Thumb-thing" Special

Creative fingerprint art is the focal point of these special Mother's Day greeting cards. In advance, prepare two shallow pans of tempera paint: one green and the other any bright color of your choice. Add a few drops of dishwashing liquid to each pan. To make a card, fold a 12" x 18" sheet of construction paper in half. Then cut out a 6" x 9" rectangle of white drawing paper and glue it to the front of the card.  Draw a small circle near the top of the paper. Have a child dip her thumb into the pan of bright-colored tempera paint. Then have her repeatedly press her thumb onto the paper around the circle to create the petals of a flower. Have her glue a length of green yarn under the flower to create a stem as shown. Ask her to dip her other thumb into the pan of green tempera paint, then press some thumbprint leaves next to the yarn stem. Have her glue a yellow or orange pom-pom atop the circle in the center of the petals. To complete her card, glue a copy of the poem on page 33 below the flower; then help each child personalize the inside of her card with a message and her signature.

Teatime Invitation

Host a special tea party to honor the special mothers (or caregivers) of your students. In advance program one copy of the tea-party invitation on page 35 with the date and time of your celebration. Then duplicate a class supply of the programmed invitation and the patterns on page 33. Have each child color and cut out the patterns and invitation. Instruct him to squeeze glue on the sides and bottom of the back of his teacup cutout only (leaving the top free from glue); then mount the cutout in the center of a sheet of 9" x 12" construction paper. Have him glue the title cloud above the teacup. Show each child how to fold his copy of the invitation in half three times—so that it is approximately the size of a tea bag. Help each youngster glue the tea-bag tags back-to-back, then tape the ends of a length of thin string to the tag and to the folded invitation, so that it resembles a tea bag. Once the glue on his teacup has dried, have each student slip his folded invitation inside it. Encourage your little ones to take their invitations home to their moms. Tea, anyone?

A Treasured Keepsake

Showcase students' masterpieces in this unique classroom art gallery that highlights mothers. In advance, collect or purchase an inexpensive picture frame for each child. Have each child draw or paint a portrait of his mother on paper sized to fit the frame. Assist him in writing or copying "My Mom" at the top of his picture; then have him write his name at the bottom. Insert each picture in its frame; then display the framed works of art in your classroom. Leave the pictures in your classroom as a decorative display for the "Teatime Party Fun!" activity (page 29), or send the pictures home as special mementos for Mother's Day.

A Corsage For Mom

Have your little ones present these special corsages to their moms on the day of your tea party (see "Teatime Party Fun!"). Help each youngster make a corsage by completing the following steps: Use colorful markers to embellish each of five paper coffee filters. Stack these filters; then pinch the stack together at the center. Bend a five-inch length of green pipe cleaner in half. Then slip the pinched portion of the filters between the open ends of the pipe cleaner. Tightly wrap a length of masking tape around the pinched filters, securing the pipe cleaner in place. Carefully pull the coffee filters apart to open the flower. Attach a large safety pin to the back of each child's completed flower, and the corsages are ready to wear!

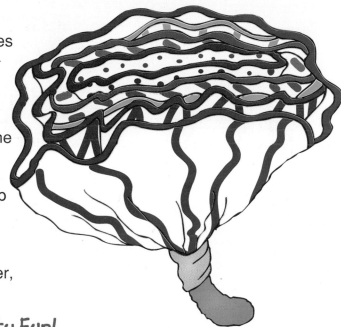

Teatime Party Fun!

It's party time—actually tea-party time! Prepare for your tea party by having little ones help you bake a batch of sugar cookies. Use heart-shaped cookie cutters and candy decorations to make the cookies extra special. Borrow a large, electric coffeepot from your school's cafeteria and fill it with water. Encourage your students to help you set up a serving table with a festive tablecloth, platters for the cookies, a sugar bowl, a pitcher of milk, and, if desired, some fresh flowers in a vase.

When the mothers have arrived, have your students sing "Welcome To Our Teatime" and present the corsages to their moms (see "A Corsage For Mom"). Have each child give her mom a tea bag to place in her special cup or mug; then let the moms fill their cups with hot water. Ask each mother to pour some of her tea (or some juice) into a thoroughly washed, play teacup for her child. Invite the mothers to prepare their tea to their liking and partake of the cookies. After the refreshments, encourage each child to present her mom with her framed portrait (see "A Treasured Keepsake" on page 28) and her Mother's Day card (see " 'Thumb-thing' Special" on page 28). What a wonderful day for some very special ladies!

Welcome To Our Teatime
(sung to the tune of "I'm A Little Teapot")

Welcome to our teatime.
We're glad you're here,
Because you are so very dear.
We hope you like the things
we've made for you...
To show how much we do love you!

Super-Duper Dads

Make dads feel special with great greetings, terrific T-shirts, splendid stories, and a sweet treat just for them!

A Handful Of Love For Dad

Invite youngsters to hand over lovely Father's Day messages with these cards. For each card, duplicate the large heart pattern on page 34 on red construction paper and the smaller heart pattern and poem boxes on white paper. Have each child trace around his own hand twice on a sheet of red construction paper; then assist him in cutting out these hand shapes, the hearts, and the poem boxes. Instruct each child to draw a self-portrait on his white heart cutout; then have him glue this white heart atop the red heart. Have each youngster cut apart the poem boxes and glue the poem on his hand cutouts as shown. Staple the hand cutouts to the top of the heart as shown; then intertwine the fingers to close the card. What a heartwarming surprise for Dad!

A Sweet Day For Dad

Plan a Doughnuts-For-Dads celebration as a sweet way for children to show their appreciation to their fathers. In advance, duplicate and program one copy of the invitation on page 35 with the date and time of your celebration; then make a copy of the invitation for each child. Have each child glue her copy of the invitation to the inside of a folded sheet of construction paper. Then help her cut out a simple doughnut shape from manila paper. Provide tempera paints, brushes, glue, and candy sprinkles.

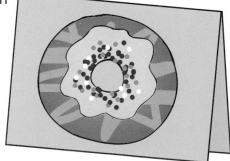

Have each child use the materials provided to decorate her doughnut cutout. When the glue and paints have dried, have her glue her doughnut to the front of the invitation. Encourage your little ones to take their invitations home and hand deliver them to their dads.

Terrific T-Shirts

Won't Dad be proud to sport this "hand-some" T-shirt? In advance ask each family to send in one adult-size, white T-shirt from home. Pour several colors of fabric paint into separate shallow containers.

Working with one or two students at a time, place a piece of cardboard or folded newspaper inside each shirt and smooth the shirt flat. Pin or tape a sheet of construction paper over the center front of each shirt. Then invite each child to press one hand into a color of paint and make handprints randomly on the front of her shirt—around the piece of paper. Have disposable wipes handy for cleanup, and encourage children to repeat this process a few times with other colors of paint.

When the paints have dried, remove the construction paper from each shirt and use a squeeze bottle of fabric paint to write the message "The Best Dad—Hands Down!" in the open space. Allow the paint to dry for a day or two. Then assist each child in wrapping her shirt in colored tissue paper. Have her present this gift to her dad during the Doughnuts-For-Dads celebration (see page 31), or send it home as a special gift.

30

Father's Day Book

Help your little ones make a meaningful Father's Day gift. To prepare a set of book covers for each child, fold and cut a sheet of 12" x 18" construction paper as shown. Help each child fold the top flaps over to make a collar for the shirt. Then have him glue the collar down securely. Invite each youngster to use crayons to draw a necktie, bow tie, pocket, or shirt design. Next staple a few 7" x 9" sheets of copy paper between the covers of each student's book. On the first page of his book, have each child write (or write for him) "I love my dad because..." and draw a picture of himself with his dad. On each of the following pages, have him illustrate special things about his dad or cut out and glue magazine pictures that depict activities he enjoys doing with his dad. Set the books aside for youngsters to share with their dads during your Doughnuts-For-Dads party.

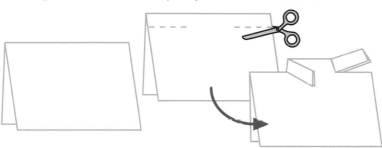

Doughnuts, Anyone?

Prior to your Doughnuts-For-Dads party, teach youngsters to recite the poem below. On the day of your celebration, borrow a large coffeepot from your school cafeteria and prepare coffee. Have little ones help you set up tables with festive table coverings and trays of assorted doughnuts and doughnut holes. In one corner of your classroom, set up a table with a manual juicer, a glass pitcher, small paper cups, and a bowl of orange halves.

As each dad arrives, have him join his child at the "juice bar" to make some freshly squeezed orange juice. Then have each child invite his dad to partake of a few doughnuts and coffee. After the refreshments, encourage each child to sit with his dad and share the book made in the "Father's Day Book" activity. Then have youngsters recite the poem they learned. At the end of the poem, have each child give his dad a big hug! Then complete this special day by having each child present the card (see "A Handful Of Love For Dad" on page 30) and T-shirt (see "Terrific T-Shirts" on page 30) that he made to his dad. A perfect end to a perfect day!

We Love Our Daddies

We love our daddies
And all that they do
To help us feel warm, safe, and snug.
We just want to say,
"Happy Father's Day!"
And to give you a great big hug!

—Linda Rice Ludlow

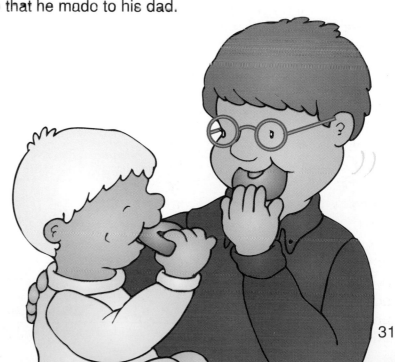

Dear Mom or Dad,

Please take a moment to help your child get to know you better. Help him or her complete the form below with information about you. We'd love a picture, too! Please return this completed form to school by _____.

(date)

Thank you for your cooperation!

Glue a picture here.

First Name: _____

Job: _____

Favorite Color: _____

Favorite Food: _____

Favorite Things To Do For Fun: _____

_____

Note To The Teacher: Use with "Getting To Know Mom And Dad" on page 27.

A Cup Of Tea For Mommy And Me!

Tea-Bag Tags

I Love You

I Love You

Mother's Day Card Poem Use with " 'Thumb-thing' Special" on page 28.

This little flower is special, you see,
Because it was made from a part of me.
My painted thumb made each flower part
To show I love you with all my heart!

Happy Mother's Day!

Father's Day Card Poem

Use with "A Handful Of Love For Dad" on page 30.

| Look inside so you can see | Who loves you best. Of course, it is ... |

ME!
Happy Father's Day !

Father's Day Card Heart Patterns

Use with "A Handful Of Love For Dad" on page 30.

You are invited to our Mother's Day Tea Party.
We hope you can come.
Please bring your favorite teacup or mug with you.

The party is on _____ at _____.
                 (date)   (time)

©1996 The Education Center, Inc. • *MAY* • TEC249

You are invited to a Doughnuts-For-Dads party.
We hope you can come.

This special celebration is on

_____ at _____.
      (date)   (time)

©1996 The Education Center, Inc. • *MAY* • TEC249

Safari Sensation

Take youngsters on an imaginary safari through the grasslands of Africa for a memorable animal adventure loaded with learning opportunities!

ideas contributed by Vicki Pacchetti and Mackie Rhodes

A-Safari We Will Go!

Do your students know what a safari is? They'll have lots of fun finding out as they learn about some of the animals that live in the grasslands of Africa. To prepare, duplicate the animal pictures on pages 44 and 45. Color the pictures; then cut out and mount each picture onto a slightly larger tagboard card. Laminate each card for durability. Attach the hook side of a piece of Velcro® to the back of each card.

Explain to students that a *safari* is a trip people take to hunt or photograph wild animals. The African grasslands are a common destination of many safaris, and participants often travel in a vehicle such as a jeep. Then introduce youngsters to some of the animals of the grasslands. Hold up each card and have youngsters name the pictured animal. Provide the name for those animals not correctly identified by students. Then place the cards on a flannelboard and teach the class this song. Invite the child whose name is used in the song to select a card from the board at the appropriate time. Ask that child to name his chosen animal, then replace the card. Repeat the song, using a different child's name each time, so that every child has the opportunity to select and name an animal.

(sung to the tune of "The Farmer In The Dell")

A-safari we will go.
A-safari we will go.
Beep! Beep! Bumpity-bump!
A-safari we will go.

[Child's name] picks an animal.
[Child's name] picks an animal.
Beep! Beep! Bumpity-bump!
[Child's name] picks an animal.

Safari Quick Facts

Use these quick facts along with the picture cards prepared in "A-Safari We Will Go!" on page 36 to provide some interesting information about grassland animals.

- The *giraffe,* with its long neck and unique coat pattern, is the tallest of all animals. It gets food from tree branches using its long tongue.

- The largest land animal, the *elephant,* uses its trunk like a hand, but can also breathe and smell with it. This animal sprays itself with water or rolls in the mud to cool off.

- The *rhinoceros*—or rhino—is a huge animal that grows one or two curvy horns from its nose and has three toes on each foot. It likes to get in the water and rest after drinking.

- The *leopard* is a type of large cat with tan fur and black spots. Being a good climber, this animal spends part of its time in trees. A black leopard is called a *panther.*

- The *hippopotamus*—or hippo—likes to spend its day resting, eating, and swimming. It can swim underwater—with its nose and ears closed—for up to six minutes.

- The *lion* has a coat the color of dead grass, which helps it to hide. It uses its 30 teeth to hold, cut, and tear its meat. Only the male lion has a mane.

- Each *zebra* has its own unique stripe pattern. It has very sharp night vision and can rotate its ears to locate sound. A baby zebra weighs 70 to 80 pounds at birth.

- The *ostrich*—the largest of all birds—has two toes on each foot. This bird can't fly, but it can run very fast. The male ostrich makes an unusual roar-hiss sound.

- The *antelope* has hollow horns that remain with it throughout its life. The most common type of antelope has a smooth coat of brown or gray hair.

- In Africa, the *buffalo* is a type of large, black, wild ox. It may spend hours soaking in a pool of water. It is known to have a bad temper and can be dangerous.

Safari Animal Masks

Invite youngsters to bring some grassland animals to life when they create these animal masks. To make a mask, provide each child with a paper plate from which an eyehole window has been cut. Encourage the student to use a variety of craft items—such as an assortment of torn and shredded paper, feathers, felt remnants, and sticker dots—to create a mask representing a grassland animal of his choice. Thread one end of a separate pipe cleaner through a hole punched on each side of the mask; then twist the pipe cleaner to secure it to the mask. Tie the loose ends of the pipe cleaners together to fit the mask to the child's head. Encourage each youngster to model his mask for his classmates as he tells about the animal it represents. Then set the masks aside for later use in "An Energized Expedition" on page 40.

A Sight To See

Not only will your little ones be seeing stripes and spots on their safari, but they'll be seeing through them as well with these animal-skin binoculars. Provide each child with a 4" x 8 1/2" sheet of construction paper. Encourage him to decorate the paper to resemble the coat of one of the animals mentioned in "Safari Quick Facts" on page 37—such as a zebra, giraffe, or leopard. Then have the child tape the paper around two toilet-paper tubes that have been stapled together to resemble a pair of binoculars. Punch holes as shown and add a length of yarn to create a carrying strap. Invite youngsters to look through their binoculars to view each flannelboard figure made in "A-Safari We Will Go!" as they sing this song. Introduce each verse of the song with the phrase, "I saw…." Repeat the song as many times as desired, each time replacing the underlined word with the name of a different grassland animal. Then have students put their binoculars aside for later use in "An Energized Expedition" on page 40.

An Ostrich On The Grassland

(sung to the tune of
"The Bear Went Over The Mountain")

I saw…
An [ostrich] on the grassland,
An [ostrich] on the grassland,
An [ostrich] on the grassland
With my binoculars!

Picture That!

A camera is a must-have when journeying through the African grasslands—and these cameras will be a snap for youngsters to make! Collect an empty, cube-shaped, facial tissue box for each child. Remove the plastic from around the opening on the box—the camera lens; then cut out a one-inch circle from the center of the box bottom to create a view hole. Invite each child to paint the outside of his box with tempera paint. After the paint dries, have him glue a foil-paper square onto one corner of the lens side of the box to represent the flash. Encourage him to glue a button onto his camera to press for picture taking. Create a camera strap by pushing an upholstery needle threaded with a length of yarn through the box on either side of the view hole. Remove the yarn from the needle; then tie a large knot in each end of the yarn.

Invite youngsters to pretend they are moving through tall grass searching for animals to photograph with their cameras. Each time the child takes a snapshot of an imaginary animal, have him illustrate that animal on a photo-sized tagboard card. Label each photo-illustration with the animal name; then display all of the photographs with the title "Picture That!" After using the cameras, set them aside for use in "An Energized Expedition" on page 40.

Elephant

Camouflaged Clothes

Invite youngsters to create camouflage safari vests before they embark on their grassland expedition. Explain to youngsters that many animals can blend in with their surroundings so that it is difficult to see them. People are also able to do this by wearing clothes that are designed to *camouflage*—or hide—the wearer. Show children an item of clothing with the popular camouflage green and brown print.

Then invite each child to make a camouflage vest. Provide several containers and paint trays, green and brown tempera paint, craft sticks for mixing, and an assortment of sponges cut into free-form shapes. Have a few volunteers mix different amounts of the tempera paints together in separate containers to create various shades of green. Pour each paint color into a separate tray. If desired, label each tray with the class-invented name for that color. To make a vest, pull the sides of a paper grocery bag outward as you flatten the bag. Then cut armholes, a front opening, and a neck hole from the bag so that it resembles a vest. Have each child sponge-paint the outside of her vest using several different sponge shapes and paint colors. Put the vests aside to dry for later use in "An Energized Expedition" on page 40.

Jiffy Jeep

Have students help create this jiffy jeep for their imaginary romp through the grasslands. Place a large appliance box—such as a stove or refrigerator box—on its side. Cut the box to resemble a jeep with door and window openings as shown. Then encourage groups of three or four youngsters to take turns painting the jeep with tempera paint in camouflage colors—such as those created in "Camouflaged Clothes." After the paint dries, attach five large, cardboard pizza rounds to the jeep—one to represent the steering wheel and the others to represent the jeep wheels. Invite each small group of children, in turn, to sit in the jeep for a bouncy pretend ride to this song. Keep the jeep available for use in dramatic play and in "An Energized Expedition" on page 40.

(sung to the tune of "Little Red Wagon")

Bumping up and down in a camouflaged jeep.
Bumping up and down in a camouflaged jeep.
Bumping up and down in a camouflaged jeep.
On a wild safari!

An Energized Expedition

It's safari time! So have your little ones gather their animal masks, binoculars, cameras, and vests made in the activities on pages 37–39. Then divide your class into groups of four students. To set up for this energized expedition, instruct the children in one group to put on their vests, then sit in the jeep with their binoculars and cameras. Have the other students put on their masks, then hide in the room. Say this chant, encouraging the students in the jeep to pat their knees in rhythm to the chant and to echo each line of the first verse. Then have them pantomime the words in the last verse. When an animal is named, invite the students wearing masks that represent that animal to come out of hiding. On a signal, have all the students return to their original positions. Repeat the chant, replacing the underlined words with a set of the provided suggestions. After several rounds of play, have the safari group switch places with an animal group. Continue in this manner until every group has had the opportunity to go on safari as well as to role-play the wild animals. To extend this activity, arrange a trip to a zoo so that students can experience real-life observations of some of these animals.

We're Going On Safari
(chanted to the rhythm of "We're Going On A Bear Hunt")

We're going on safari
To see what we can see.
We've got our cameras
And binoculars, too!

Uh-oh! There's an [elephant].
A [huge elephant]!
We can't go near it—
We don't want to scare it.
Look through your binoculars.
Take a picture, too.

Each time the verse is repeated, replace the underlined words with one of the following sets of words:

giraffe; tall giraffe
lion; fierce lion
leopard; wild leopard
hippo; hungry hippo
ostrich; large ostrich
zebra; fast zebra
rhino; lazy rhino
antelope; handsome antelope
buffalo; angry buffalo

Learning Skills, Safari-Style

Multiply the learning fun by duplicating a supply of the animal pictures on pages 44 and 45 to use in these activities, including a booklet about safari animals.

Safari Animal Sort

Promote critical-thinking skills in your youngsters with this sorting game. Prepare a set of animal pictures as described in "A-Safari We Will Go!" on page 36 (wihout the Velcro®, if desired). Group the cards according to characteristics shared by each animal—such as by coat design, number of legs, or presence of horns. Encourage youngsters to determine what common characteristic is shared by the animals In each group.

Safari Animals At Home

Invite youngsters to take some safari animals home with them. To prepare, duplicate the parent letter on page 45 for each child. Then give each child a set of the animal pictures to color and cut out. Have him put his pictures in a resealable plastic bag with a copy of the parent letter. Encourage each child to take home his bag of pictures to share with his family.

My Safari Booklet

Sum up your grassland adventure with these individual booklets. For each child, duplicate the booklet cover and pages found on pages 42 and 43 on white construction paper. Have each child complete each page following the provided suggestions. Then have him cut apart, sequence, and bind his pages behind the booklet cover.

Booklet Cover: Write your name on the line.
Page 1: Glue wiggle eyes on the Xs; then cover the page with artificial grass.
Page 2: Color tho giraffe. Glue tissue-paper leaves onto the tree.
Page 3: Color the hippo. Use a blue glitter crayon to color the water.
Page 4: Color the elephant. Cotton-paint brown mud on and around the elephant.
Page 5: Color the leopard yellow. Use small sticker dots for its spots.
Page 6: Color the rhino. Glue a macaroni horn on Its nose.
Page 7: Color the picture. Glue a foil-paper flash on the camera.

My Safari Booklet

by _____

x   x

Off on safari. Here we go!
Searching for animals high
and low.

1

Look! A giraffe eating leaves
off trees.

2

There's a hippo swimming
'round with ease.

3

See the elephant cooling off in the mud. 4

And the leopard jumping down with a *thud!* 5

Here comes a rhino with a horn on his nose. 6

And that's me with my camera, snapping each pose! 7

Animal Pictures

Use with "A-Safari We Will Go!" on page 36, and "Safari Animal Sort" and "Safari Animals At Home" on page 41.

elephant

leopard

giraffe

zebra

ostrich

hippopotamus

Animal Pictures

Use with "A-Safari We Will Go!" on page 36, and "Safari Animal Sort" and "Safari Animals At Home" on page 41.

rhinoceros

antelope

buffalo

lion

Parent Letter

Use with "Safari Animals At Home" on page 41.

Dear Parent,

Our class has just returned from an imaginary safari to the grasslands of Africa. Please take some time to have your child name each of the animals on the enclosed cards. Ask your child to tell you something he or she has learned about each animal.

Thank you for supporting your child's learning!

Dig Into These Delights! Rocks, Dirt, And Mud

Ready to get down and dirty? Roll up your sleeves and dig into this ooey, gooey unit featuring hands-on investigations to help you and your little ones get the scoop on rocks, dirt, and mud.

ideas contributed by Suzanne Moore and Sharon Murphy

On A Hunt—For Rocks!

Introduce your youngsters to the topic of rocks with a rock hunt. Plan to take your rock hounds for a walk on your school grounds, around your school's neighborhood, or to a local park. For each child, provide a resealable plastic bag containing a plastic spoon and a craft stick. During the walk, invite youngsters to use their materials to dig and collect three rocks. Encourage children to choose rocks that will be lightweight enough for them to carry. If rocks are not accessible near your school, purchase a bag of landscaping pebbles at your local home-improvement store; then scatter them near your classroom for your students to find.

When you return from the rock hunt, have each child choose one of his three rocks as his favorite. Ask students to keep their favorite rocks in their plastic bags and set the other rocks aside to use in the activity "Investigation At The Rock Station." Attach a copy of the observation report (page 50) to each child's plastic bag. Ask him to complete the report at home with a parent's help and then return it to school. When all the rocks and finished reports have been returned, invite each student to describe his rock. Challenge your rock hounds to comment on the similarities and differences among their rocks.

Investigation At The Rock Station

Now that your rock hounds have rounded up some rocks, it's time to investigate. Display several rocks that you have collected and ask your little ones to think of words that describe them—such as *big, little, shiny, dull, smooth, bumpy, heavy,* and *light.* Record the children's responses on a piece of chart paper and display the list on a classroom wall.

Next set up a rock station or center in your classroom using the extra rocks gathered on the rock hunt. Provide balance scales, counters, and rulers for measuring the rocks; magnifying glasses for examining the rocks; and paper and pencils for students to use for recording their observations. Invite small groups of students to closely inspect the rocks at the station. Also provide a small tub of water into which students can dip the rocks and observe any changes. For a final activity at the station, label several Styrofoam® meat trays with various attributes of rocks. Encourage youngsters to sort the rocks onto the trays.

Barry Slate

FLAT   SHINY   HEAVY

Magic Pebbles

Delight your little ones when you present them with their own pebbles after reading *Sylvester And The Magic Pebble* by William Steig (Simon & Schuster Books For Young Readers). In advance purchase a small bag of purple aquarium pebbles. After reading the story, ask each student what she would wish for if she had a magic pebble. Then provide each child with a 9" x 12" sheet of construction paper and one purple aquarium pebble. In one corner of the paper, have each child trace around one hand and then glue her pebble inside the outline. At the top of her paper, have each child illustrate her wish and encircle it with a cloud shape. Have the child explain why she chose that wish. Write her dictation below her picture. Staple all the completed pages between construction-paper covers. Print the title "Magic Pebble Wishes" on the front cover. Read the finished book to the class; then add it to your classroom library for some magical reading!

Patti

I wish I could drive a car because that's fun.

Rock Rhythms

Your students will be ready to rock 'n' roll once they learn that rocks make great rhythm instruments! Invite your youngsters to make their own instruments by tapping rocks together, tapping them on the floor, or shaking potato-chip cans full of small pebbles. After each student has decided on an instrument, teach the class this chant and have them accompany it with instruments.

Rock Chant

Rocks are found	(tap, tap)
All around.	(tap, tap)
Under the ocean,	(tap, tap)
And in the ground.	(tap, tap)
Some are big.	(Continue to tap
Some are small.	or shake rocks
Some are even	two times after
Very tall.	each line.)

Rocks are used
For many things.
Chalk and roads,
And stones in rings.

Bridges and buildings,
A fireplace, too.
I'm sure rocks are found
Somewhere near you!

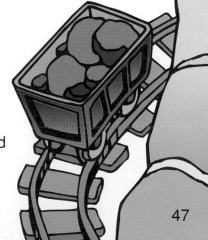

It's Dirt Day!

Get out those shovels! It's time for your little ones to do some real hands-on exploring—right in the dirt and mud! Plan a fun-filled "Dirt Day." First program one copy of the parent letter on page 50 with the date of your Dirt Day. Then send home a copy of the programmed letter with each child in your class. Then dress for the day yourself in old clothing. The activities on these two pages can be set up for the whole class or as small-group stations. You'll probably want to set up the activities outside and ask for the help of a few teaching assistants or parent volunteers.

Bring On The Dirt!

You will definitely need your youngsters' help for this activity. In advance ask permission to dig up some dirt on your school grounds. Distribute small shovels and buckets to your students. Invite them to help you dig dirt from a designated area to fill up a baby pool and your sensory table. These activities require plenty of dirt to delve into!

Dirt, Wonderful, Dirt

Now that you've got all this dirt, send your students exploring! Set up the dirt-filled baby pool as an exploration area. To do this, add colanders, spoons, measuring cups, hand shovels, and magnifying glasses. Your little ones will love the chance to dig and explore in the dirt.

If you're adventurous, invite your youngsters to do some "dirty dancing." Have them take off their shoes and tromp through the dirt in their bare feet. Of course, you'll want to have a big tub of water and some old towels available for cleanup.

A Delightful Dirt Paperweight

Encourage little ones to create special paperweights for parents. In advance bring in at least three different colors of soil—such as sand, potting soil, and red clay dirt. Place each type of soil in a large container; then add a few plastic spoons to each container. To make a paperweight, provide each child with a baby-food jar (with the label removed). Have him spoon a layer of sand in the bottom of his jar, then tap the jar firmly on a tabletop to remove any air bubbles. Next have him spoon a layer of potting soil on top of the sand and tap the jar again. Then have him add a layer of red clay on top of the potting soil so that it fills the jar, again remembering to tap it firmly to get rid of any air bubbles. When the jar is filled to the very top, assist the child in tightly sealing the lid on his jar.

To personalize the paperweights, provide each child with a 3 1/2-inch circle of fabric. Have him glue the fabric circle on the top of his lid and secure it with a rubber band. Duplicate a copy of the following poem for each child. Have him sign his name at the bottom, then attach the poem to the jar with tape. Then have each student take the gift home for a dirt-filled, but much treasured keepsake.

Dear Mom and Dad,
Sometimes when I'm having fun,
You have to clean up when I'm done.
I track in mud and drag in dirt.
It's on my hands, my feet, my shirt.
Mud on the carpet, mud on the floors,
Dirt in the kitchen, dirt on the doors.
This dirt I bring to you today,
Won't make a mess in any way.
Set this jar where you can see,
To make you think of messy me!
Love,
Taylor

Adobe Bricks

For centuries people have been putting dirt to good use as a building material. Make adobe bricks—a building material made of sun-dried earth and straw—to give your little ones the chance to see just how useful dirt can be! To make adobe bricks with a small group, add water to two cups of soil until you have a thick mixture of mud. Next have students use safety scissors to cut straw into small pieces. Add sand and pieces of straw to the mud. Invite students to take turns mixing the mixture with their hands until it is very stiff, yet still moldable. (The amounts of water, straw, and sand needed will vary depending on the type of soil and sand you use.) Pour the mixture into plastic ice-cube trays or small jewelry boxes and pack the mud down tightly to eliminate all air pockets. Drying time varies—from a few days to up to three weeks—depending on the humidity in your area. To test the bricks for dryness, drop one; if it breaks, the inside of the brick is not completely dry. Once the bricks have dried, encourage students to build some adobe structures.

Mud Pie Bakery

Order up—mud pies for sale! Delight your youngsters with the chance to make mud pies as they experiment with a favorite childhood recipe, "dirt + water = mud." Invite students to add water to the soil in your sensory table until they make mud. Provide aluminum pie pans, plastic spoons, bowls, and measuring cups for students to play with in the mud and make mud pies. Supply old aprons for your little chefs to wear as they whip up these delicacies. For a final touch, display a sign advertising these one-of-a-kind pies!

Delicious Mud

Once your little chefs have made a supply of mud pies, they will surely be ready for some *truly* edible mud. Invite your youngsters to wash up; then use the recipe to make a delectable dessert of mud.

Delicious Mud
(serves 1)
3 Tbsp. instant chocolate pudding
1/2 cup milk
2 chocolate sandwich cookies

Place the cookies in a resealable plastic bag. Use your hands to break the cookies into tiny bits. Pour the milk and the pudding mix into a small jar or a margarine tub with a tight-fitting lid. Shake for three minutes. Pour the pudding (mud) into a clear plastic cup. Sprinkle the cookie bits (dirt) on top of the mud. Dig in!

Dig Into A Good Book

Milk Rock
Written by John Kaufman
Published by Henry Holt & Company, Inc.

Stone Soup
Written by Ann McGovern
Published by Scholastic Inc.

The Piggy In The Puddle
Written by Charlotte Pomerantz
Published by Aladdin Books

The Mud Pony: A Traditional Skidi Pawnee Tale
Adapted by Caron Lee Cohen
Published by Scholastic Inc.

Observation Report
Use with "On A Hunt—For Rocks!" on page 46.

Dear Family,

   We went on a rock hunt today. Please help me complete the report below using the rock I brought home. I need to return the rock and the finished report to school tomorrow.

Name _____

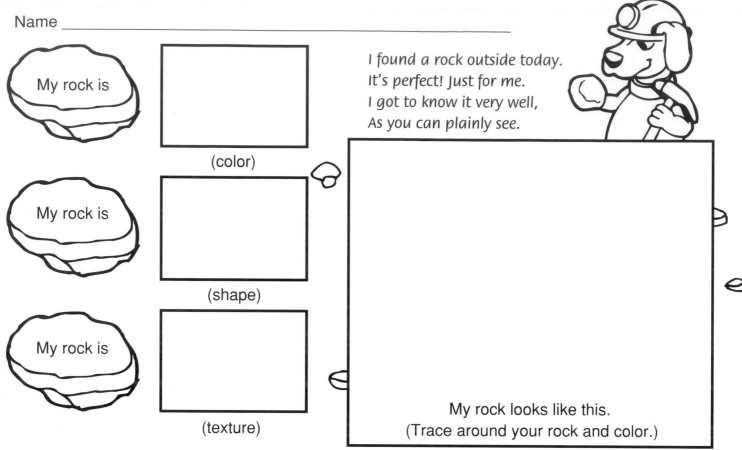

My rock is

(color)

My rock is

(shape)

My rock is

(texture)

I found a rock outside today.
It's perfect! Just for me.
I got to know it very well,
As you can plainly see.

My rock looks like this.
(Trace around your rock and color.)

Parent Letter
Use with "It's Dirt Day!" on page 48.

Dear Parent,

   Our class has been learning about rocks, dirt, and mud. We will be having a special **Dirt Day** at school on _____.
   (date)
Please send your child to school that day wearing old clothes and ready to get down and dirty in the mud! He or she should bring an extra set of clothing to change into after the activities have been completed.

Thank you!

_____
(teacher signature)

Magnets— What's The Attraction?

Little ones love the magic of magnets! Attract their attention with this collection of developmentally appropriate magnet activities. Your youngsters' fascination with magnets will grow, and they will be drawn to investigate magnets on their own.

ideas contributed by Lucia Kemp Henry and Sue Hohbach

Pulling It Together

To make this exploration unit a success, have on hand a collection of magnetic manipulatives. Check your school's resource room or your local teacher supply store for magnet exploration kits. Magnets come in many shapes—such as horseshoe, marble, wand, bar, and doughnut. Gather magnets in a variety of shapes and strengths to add interest to the activities that follow.

Is It Magnetic?

Provide an opportunity for your little ones to experiment with magnets by creating an exploration center in your classroom. Encourage your youngsters to test the magnetic attraction of an assortment of objects. Place several magnets and a collection of magnetic and nonmagnetic objects in the center (see list for suggestions). Enlarge and duplicate the sorting sheet on page 55 for your little scientists to use to record their findings. After a student tests an object's ability to stick to a magnet, ask him to place it on the appropriate section of the sorting sheet. The magnetism of this center will captivate your young learners. They will be drawn to this hands-on activity again and again!

After some exploration, invite youngsters to learn more about magnets when you share the simple book *The Mystery Of Magnets* by Melvin Berger (Newbridge Communications, Inc.). This book can be ordered directly from Newbridge at 1-800-867-0307.

Is It Magnetic?

Yes 😊	No ☹

Magnetic	**Nonmagnetic**
paper clips	wooden block
nuts and bolts	aluminum foil
blunt scissors	seashell
metal washers	rock
metal spoon	plastic spoon
metal key ring	coin

Spinning Magnet Dancers

Children are amazed by a magnet's strength in attracting metal objects. Use this fun activity to show your students that magnets have the ability to attract metal objects through paper.

Set up a paper dance floor by taping a sheet of tagboard to two rectangular wooden blocks as shown. Then make a few magnet dancers. For each dancer, simply hot-glue a plastic, animal-shaped counter (such as a bear or dinosaur) to the inside of a plastic milk-jug lid. Then hot-glue a paper clip to the bottom of the jug lid.

Then let the dancing begin! Place the magnet dancers on the dance floor. Then play or sing some of your youngsters' favorite songs while students take turns moving a magnet under the tagboard. The magnet dancers will spin and glide across the dance floor to the delight of your little ones!

Magic Flying Butterfly

Delight your youngsters with this amazing flying butterfly trick to demonstrate another magnet trait—magnetic attraction through air. You will need a clean, empty baby-food jar with a lid. Also gather a magnet (that will fit under the lid of the jar), a small metal paper clip, a 1" x 2" scrap of tissue paper, a four-inch length of thread, and tape. Place the magnet inside the lid and secure it with tape if necessary. Tie one end of the thread to one end of the paper clip and insert the tissue paper into the paper clip to resemble a butterfly's wings. Then tape the loose thread to the inside bottom of the jar. (When you pull the butterfly up, it should not quite reach the top of the jar.)

To perform the trick for your little ones, show them the uncovered jar containing the "sleeping" butterfly. Tell students that you will wake up the butterfly and make him fly. Then place the lid on the jar, turn it upside down, and then turn it upright again. Youngsters will be amazed to see the butterfly "fluttering" inside the jar, suspended just below the jar's lid. Reveal the magnet on the jar lid and discuss how the magnet attracted the paper clip. Point out that the magnet is able to attract the paper-clip butterfly even when some space (air) is left between them. Then place the jar in your science center for students to experiment with on their own.

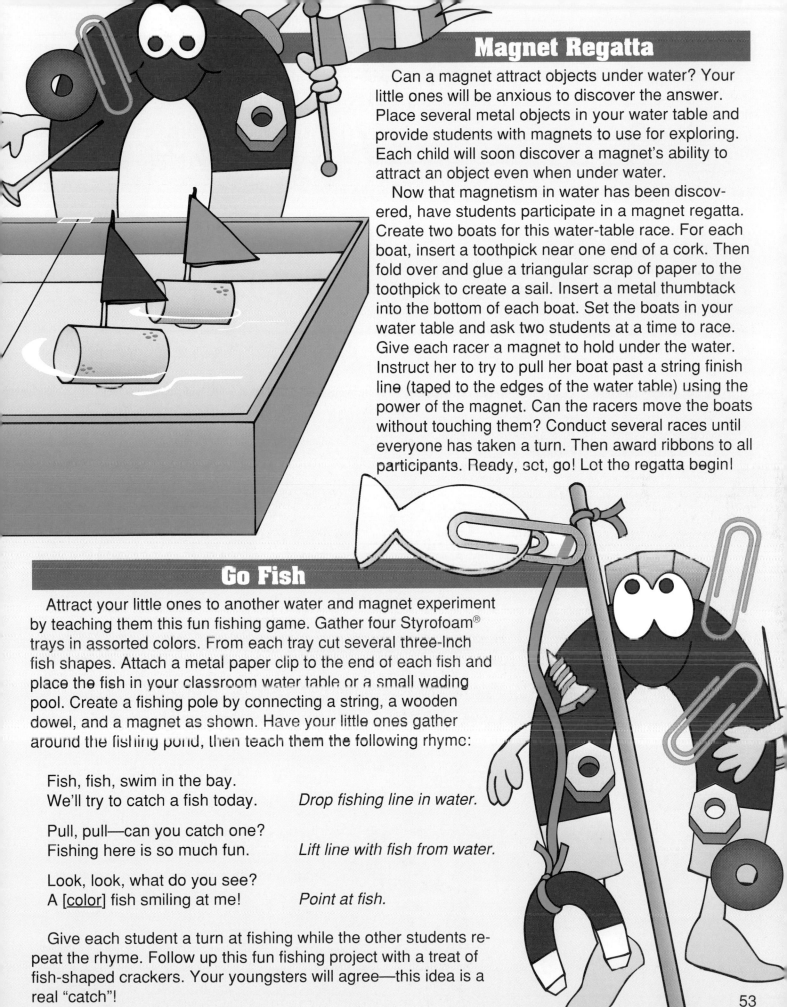

Magnet Regatta

Can a magnet attract objects under water? Your little ones will be anxious to discover the answer. Place several metal objects in your water table and provide students with magnets to use for exploring. Each child will soon discover a magnet's ability to attract an object even when under water.

Now that magnetism in water has been discovered, have students participate in a magnet regatta. Create two boats for this water-table race. For each boat, insert a toothpick near one end of a cork. Then fold over and glue a triangular scrap of paper to the toothpick to create a sail. Insert a metal thumbtack into the bottom of each boat. Set the boats in your water table and ask two students at a time to race. Give each racer a magnet to hold under the water. Instruct her to try to pull her boat past a string finish line (taped to the edges of the water table) using the power of the magnet. Can the racers move the boats without touching them? Conduct several races until everyone has taken a turn. Then award ribbons to all participants. Ready, set, go! Let the regatta begin!

Go Fish

Attract your little ones to another water and magnet experiment by teaching them this fun fishing game. Gather four Styrofoam® trays in assorted colors. From each tray cut several three-inch fish shapes. Attach a metal paper clip to the end of each fish and place the fish in your classroom water table or a small wading pool. Create a fishing pole by connecting a string, a wooden dowel, and a magnet as shown. Have your little ones gather around the fishing pond, then teach them the following rhyme:

Fish, fish, swim in the bay.
We'll try to catch a fish today.   *Drop fishing line in water.*

Pull, pull—can you catch one?
Fishing here is so much fun.   *Lift line with fish from water.*

Look, look, what do you see?
A [color] fish smiling at me!   *Point at fish.*

Give each student a turn at fishing while the other students repeat the rhyme. Follow up this fun fishing project with a treat of fish-shaped crackers. Your youngsters will agree—this idea is a real "catch"!

53

Magnetic Long Jump

This activity really measures up when it comes to determining a magnet's strength. Help your little ones investigate the pulling power of several magnets. Set up a magnetic long jump at a classroom exploration center. Tape a ruler to a tabletop; then have a student place a paper clip on the table near the left end of the ruler as shown. Next gather an assortment of magnets and have a child place one magnet near the right end of the ruler. Have the student slowly push the magnet toward the paper clip until the paper clip attaches to the magnet. To record the distance, move the magnet to the other side of the ruler at the point where the paper clip attached. Return the paper clip to the left end of the ruler, and repeat the experiment using a different magnet. When the test is complete, the lineup of magnets will indicate their strengths from weakest to strongest. Which magnet is the long-jump champ?

Pam Crane

Make A Magnet Gift

Refrigerators all over town will be more attractive when your little ones bring home these delightful magnets! To prepare, cut a class supply of three-inch circles from poster board. Also cut a large supply of felt flower petals in a variety of bright colors. Then cut a photocopy of each child's school picture into a 1 1/2-inch circle. Ask each student to glue her picture to the center of the poster-board circle, and then select several petals to glue around the edge of the picture as shown. After the glue has dried, attach a green pipe-cleaner stem and a magnetic strip to the back of the flower. Your classroom will be blooming with smiles when this project is finished!

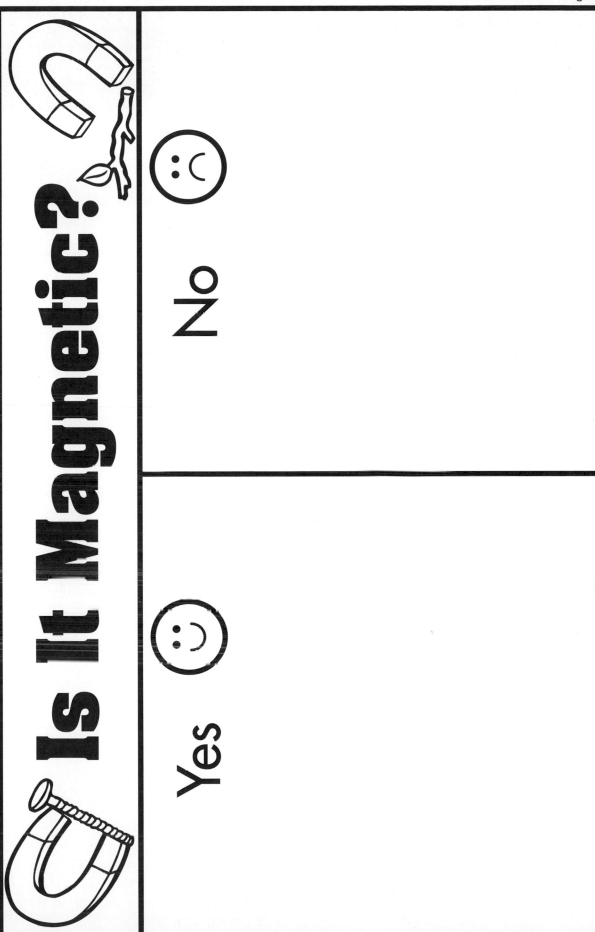

Is It Magnetic?

No

Yes

©1996 The Education Center, Inc. • *MAY* • TEC249

"Bee-utiful" Bees

The buzzword in this unit is *bees*. Youngsters will swarm to your classroom to take part in these exciting, integrated activities.

ideas contributed by Linda Gordetsky and Angie Kutzer

Bring On The Bees

A recording of Rimsky-Korsakov's "Flight Of The Bumblebee" and some active imaginations are all you need to introduce this unit to your students. (This classical recording can be found on the compact disc *Nature And Make-Believe* from the New Bowmar Orchestral Series I. To order call 1-800-438-1637.) Play the recording, and have youngsters sit with their eyes closed and imagine that they are bees. Ask questions about what they are doing as bees when the music is slow and again as the music gets faster. Play the music again and invite your little ones to buzz around the room searching for imaginary flowers. Afterward show bee illustrations from reference books and share the bee facts below.

It's "Un-bee-lievable"!

- There are no bees near the North and South poles.
- *Worker bees* are females and *drone bees* are males.
- Only female bees have stings.
- Several worker bees guard the entrance to the hive and sting when the hive is in danger.
- Bees can see colors, but cannot see the color red.
- Bees use their antennae to smell.
- A bee has a special stomach, called a *honey stomach,* that carries nectar.
- A bee can fly forward, backward, or sideways, and it can hover in the air.

"Bee-ware" Of The Bear!

Wings flap, eyes move, and a big bear gets stung as your curious listeners enjoy facts and fiction in Eric Carle's *The Honeybee And The Robber: A Moving Picture Book* (Scholastic Inc.). After sharing the story, surprise your youngsters with the flannelboard pieces from page 63. First make a copy of page 64 for later use; then cut out the story pieces from page 63. Laminate the pieces and attach a strip of felt to the back of each piece. Have your little honeys use these flannelboard characters to tell the story in their own words as they recall the sequence of events.

Guarding The Hive

Invite youngsters to imitate worker bees guarding the hive in this fun game. Gather a beanbag for each child and create a simple, brown, construction-paper headband. Buzz out to the playground and divide your class into two equal groups. Arrange the groups in two lines—about 20 feet apart—so that they are facing each other. Designate one line as the Bees and give each Bee a beanbag to represent honey. Designate the other line as the Bears.

To play the game, place the headband on a Bear's head. The Bees insert this child's name and chant, "[Child's name] Bear, [Child's name] Bear, leave our honey alone." The designated Bear chants, "Here I come. Here I come. Honey, honey, yum, yum, YUM!" All the Bees turn away from the Bear line and hold their honey behind them. Then the designated Bear runs to the Bee line and takes the honey from one Bee. That Bee then chases the Bear back to the Bear line and tries to tag him. If the Bear is stung (tagged), he becomes a Bee and joins the Bee line. If the Bear is not tagged, he returns to the Bear line, and the Bee becomes a Bear. Stop the game periodically to have your students count and compare the two lines. Continue this game of honey snatching until interest fades.

Work, Work, Work

Guarding the entrance to the hive is not the only job of a worker bee. Teach your little ones other worker-bee tasks by using this action song.

(sung to the tune of "She'll Be Coming 'Round The Mountain")

They'll be flying 'round the flowers in the yard. Buzz, buzz!   *(Flap hands.)*
They'll be flying 'round the flowers in the yard. Buzz, buzz!
They'll be flying 'round the flowers; they'll be flying round the flowers;
They'll be flying 'round the flowers in the yard. Buzz, buzz!

Repeat the song several times—substituting one of the following lines each time:

They'll be slurping up the nectar when they come. Gulp, gulp!   *(Pretend to swallow.)*
They'll be scooping up the pollen with their legs. Fun, fun!   *(Stomp twice.)*
They'll be feeding all the babies in the hive. Eat, eat!   *(Pretend to rock baby.)*
They'll be cooling down the hive with their wings. Flap, flap!   *(Flap arms.)*
They'll be making lots of honey that we'll eat. Yum, yum!   *(Rub tummy.)*

Follow My Lead

Bees communicate with their bodies. When a scout has found a food source for the hive, she returns and performs a dance that tells other bees the direction and distance of the food. Her movements are precise and vigorous. Soon other members of the hive join her, imitating her movements.

Assist your group in forming a circle. Play some "bee-bopping" music while a volunteer dances in the center of the circle. Have the rest of the class imitate his movements; then let another scout take center stage!

Hexagons And Honey

Help your students make this honey of a treat! Each child will need seven Harvest Crisps® 5-Grain baked snack crackers and a Styrofoam® plate. You will also need a squeeze bottle full of honey.

Use a reference book to help your children learn how honey is made. Show them several pictures of *honeycombs* and *hives.* Inform children that a honeycomb is made of individual cells and that each of these cells has six sides. Explain that a six-sided shape is called a *hexagon.* Then explain that when workers bring nectar back to the hive, they put it in these hexagon cells. Other worker bees in the hive add substances from their bodies to turn the nectar into honey.

To construct this edible hive, squirt enough honey onto each child's plate so that the inner circle is sparsely covered. Hold up one cracker and have your youngsters count each side as you point to it. Then distribute the crackers.

Have each child lay one of her crackers in her honey; then instruct her to turn the cracker over and place it in the center of her plate. Direct her to do the same thing with the rest of the crackers—positioning each of them with one of their sides touching a side of the center cracker as shown. Then invite each youngster to "dive" into her hive. Don't be surprised to see lots of finger licking!

Queen For A Game

After making the ooey-gooey snack described in "Hexagons And Honey" (page 58), reinforce students' shape-recognition skills with this fun card game. To prepare, make three construction-paper copies of the shape cards on page 62 and cut apart the cards. You will also need to make a simple construction-paper crown.

This game for two players begins by shuffling the cards and placing them facedown in a basket. Have each child, in turn, pick a card. If the player chooses a card with a honeycomb-shaped hexagon, have the child lay it in front of her. If the card does not show a hexagon, direct her to deposit it in another basket for discards. The first child to draw four hexagons is the queen bee and gets to wear the crown for the next round. Have the children shuffle the cards and begin again. Pass the crown to the queen bee of each round. What a good deal!

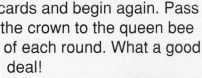

Wax Magic

Your little ones will be surprised to know that bees are useful not only for making honey, but also for making wax. Explain that bees use their wax to build honeycomb cells and to seal these cells once honey is stored inside. Inform your children that people use *beeswax* in candles, lipsticks, polishes, and waterproofing compounds. Reveal that wax has a special quality that doesn't allow water to go through it. Give each child a piece of white paper and a piece of Gulfwax®. Invite him to draw a picture on the paper with the wax, then to paint over it with watercolors. Like magic, the wax resists the water, and the invisible picture suddenly appears. Ta-da!

In And Out Of Flowers

This fine-motor activity is perfect for busy little hands. Copy the sewing card on page 64 onto card stock for each child. Then have him color his card. Punch a hole through the middle of each flower and the hive. Tape the knotted end of a 24-inch piece of yarn to the back of the card at the first flower by the bee; then wrap tape around the other end of the yarn to make it stiff. Encourage the child to use the yarn to trace the bee's path in and out of the flowers to end up at the hive. Collecting nectar and pollen is "sew" much fun!

59

Pollen Path

Numeral-recognition and counting skills will be reinforced when your busy bees play this interactive-display game.

To Prepare:
1. Draw a curving path onto a bulletin board as shown and label "Start".
2. Have each child draw, color, and cut out a flower from a 4" x 5" piece of construction paper.
3. Cut the same number of yellow construction-paper circles (pollen) as the number of student-made flowers.
4. Make several bee game markers by duplicating the pattern from the card on page 64. Color each bee so that it is distinguishable from the others.
5. Laminate the flowers, pollen circles, and bee game markers.
6. Attach the hook side of a Velcro® dot to each of the flower centers.
7. Attach the loop side of a Velcro® dot to the back of each pollen circle and bee.
8. Mount the flowers along the path using pushpins.
9. Stick a pollen circle to each flower.
10. Label 20 index cards: two each with a different numeral from one to ten. Mix up the cards and store them in a paper lunch bag near the bulletin board.

Directions For Players:
1. Choose a bee game marker and begin at "Start".
2. Pick a numeral card.
3. Count the corresponding number of flowers from "Start".
4. If you land on a flower with pollen, remove the pollen and place your bee on the flower.
5. If there is no pollen, place your bee on the flower.
6. Continue taking turns until there is no more pollen.
7. The person (bee) who collected the most pollen gets to reset the board for the next swarm of players.

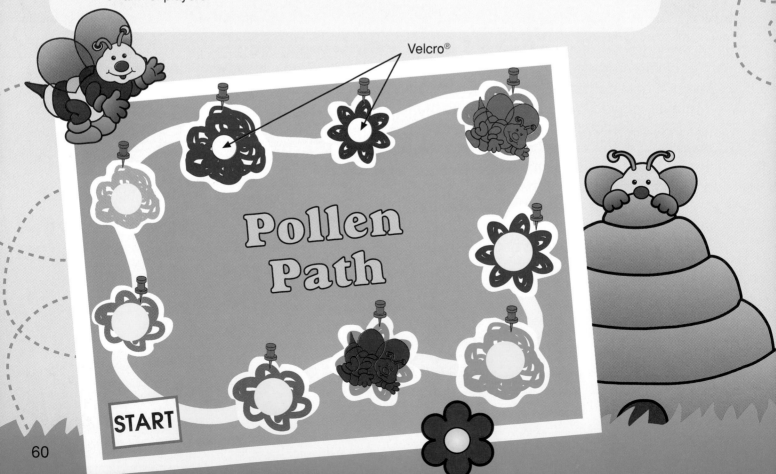

Velcro®

Pollen Path

START

Our Busy Bee Book

Encourage your young authors to try their wings at making a page for this classroom book. First read the story *Honeybee's Busy Day* by Richard Fowler (Doubleday); then ask students to recall all of the places Honeybee traveled and the characters he met. Then, as a group, brainstorm and list other places he could go and different animals and distractions he could buzz into. Give each child a sheet of paper, and have her illustrate an idea from the list or her own idea. On the first page of your classroom book, write "Honeybee was busy finding nectar to make honey when…." Then complete this sentence by writing each child's dictation on her individual page. Duplicate the bee from the sewing card on page 64 on tagboard and cut it out. Laminate the bee and the pages of the book. Use a scrap of laminating film to make a hexagonal flap for the last page of the book. Cut a slit in each page with an X-acto® knife; then bind all the pages together on the left-hand side. Honeybee's ready to take flight. Buzz, buzz!

The Buzz On Bees

Give your students a chance to show what they know about bees. Invite student volunteers to tell you something they have learned about bees during this unit. Write each child's statement on a sheet of chart paper along with her name. Display the chart in your classroom, and transfer the responses and names onto a copy of the newsletter form on page 65. Then reproduce the newsletter for each child to take home and share with her family. Parents will "bee" excited to read their children's contributions!

Need More Information?

Make a beeline to the library! Share the pictures and summarize some text from one or more of these nonfiction books on bees.

The Fascinating World Of…Bees
Written by Angels Julivert
Published by Forest House Publishing Co., Inc.

The Life Cycle Of The Honeybee
Written by Paula Z. Hogan
Published by Raintree Children's Books

The Bee: Friend Of The Flowers
Written by Paul Starosta
Published by Charlesbridge Publishing

Busy As A Bee
Written by Melvin Berger
Published by Newbridge Communications, Inc.
(This book can be ordered from Newbridge at 1-800-867-0307.)

Shape Cards

Use with "Queen For A Game" on page 59.

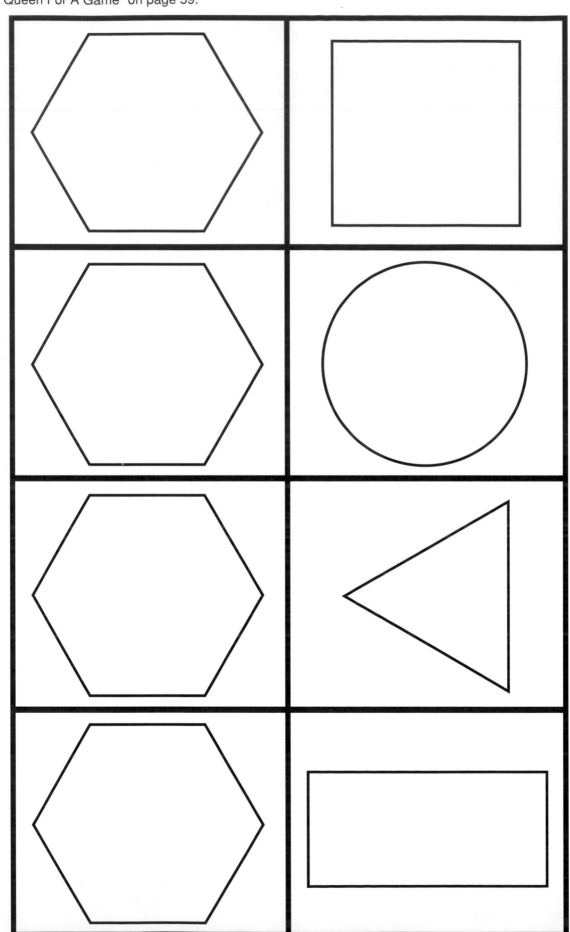

Sewing Card

Use with "In And Out Of Flowers" on page 59.
Use the bee with "Pollen Path" on page 60 and "Our Busy Bee Book" on page 61.

The BUZZ On Bees

Dear Family,

We have finished our unit on bees. You won't "bee-lieve" how much we've learned! Listed "bee-low" are some interesting comments that were contributed by our roving reporters during our final activity. Read all about it!

A Rootin'-Tootin' Good Time

Saddle up and hold on tight! We're headin' west in this unit! Cowboys and cowgirls everywhere will hoot and holler when this unit rolls into town. Help your little ones experience the Wild West with this roundup of hands-on activities that gallop across the curriculum. Yee-ha!

ideas contributed by Lucia Kemp Henry and Angie Kutzer

Westward, Ho!

Prepare your little ones for their journey west by sharing the book *Gila Monsters Meet You At The Airport* by Marjorie Weinman Sharmat (Macmillan Publishing Company). After reading the story, ask your students why the boy was surprised once he arrived out West. Explain that while there's not much difference between the West and other parts of the United States today, a long time ago things were very different. Inform your youngsters that they will be taking an imaginary trip back to the Old West of long ago. Back then, pioneers thought May was the perfect time to set out because the spring rains had ended, the grass was plentiful, and there was just enough time to get over the mountains before the heavy snowfalls.

Wild West Duds

Outfit your posse with the typical accessories of the West. Use the directions below to help your youngsters make hats and bandanas with a western flair.

Headband Hats: A cowboy hat was essential. It kept rain, snow, and sun off the cowboy's face, and was also useful for fanning fires and signaling to others. Make full-size hat patterns from old file folders by using the pattern on page 72. Have each child trace one of these hat patterns onto colored construction paper. Then have her cut out the hat shape and decorate it as desired. Center her cutout on a sentence strip; then staple the middle of the cutout to the strip. Fit each youngster's headband to her head; then staple the ends of the strip together.

Bold Bandanas: A cowboy would usually wear a bandana tied around his neck so that it could be pulled over his nose during a ride on a dry, dusty trail. Cut red and blue bandana fabric into large squares. Assist each child with writing his name with dimensional fabric paint on his bandana. When the paint is dry, tie his bandana around his neck. Now he's ready for the next dust storm!

Rollin', Rollin', Rollin'

Present this problem for your little wranglers to solve: "No trains, planes, or cars. How are we going to travel to the Old West?" Inform your group that *covered wagons* were the best way to move families and belongings during this time of expansion. Cite interesting facts and show the illustrations from *...If You Traveled West In A Covered Wagon* by Ellen Levine (Scholastic Inc.). Or—if you can't obtain this book—share some "Wagon Wisdom" with your students.

Wagon Wisdom

- A wagon was made of wood and covered with a piece of white canvas.
- The wagon's canvas could be pulled tight on the ends to keep out dust, wind, and rain.
- Covered wagons were also called *prairie schooners*.
- Oxen pulled the wagons because they were stronger and cheaper than horses or mules.
- *Wagon trains* were formed for better protection against Indian attacks and bandits.
- The wagons would travel in a line during the day.
- At night the settlers would form a circle with the wagons.

My Own Covered Wagon

Your youngsters will be ready to get a move on after constructing these miniature replicas of covered wagons. To prepare, gather the following materials: individual serving-size cereal boxes, an X-acto® knife (optional), brass fasteners, Styrofoam® meat trays, 4" x 9" strips of white construction paper, brown paint, yarn, and a hole puncher. Cut four, two-inch circles from the meat trays for each child. Cut off the front panel of each cereal box with scissors or an X-acto® knife. To make holes for wheels, punch four holes in each of the cereal boxes—at least 1/2 inch from the bottom and sides of the box.

To make a covered wagon, have each child paint the outside of his box brown. When the paint is dry, assist him in completing the following steps:

1. Staple an end of a paper strip to each side of the box as shown.
2. Poke a brad through the middle of each wheel.
3. Connect the wheels to the wagon by inserting the brads through the holes and loosely opening the metal arms.
4. Tape one end of a length of yarn to the front of the wagon.

Here We Go!

With your pioneers in a straight line and their wagons alongside, lead your wagon train around the room. Have your little ones join you in singing this song as you pretend to wind through mountains, across rivers, and over prairies.

(sung to the tune of "Go In And Out The Window")
We're in a covered wagon.
We're in a covered wagon.
We're in a covered wagon,
A-rollin' down the trail!

We're in a covered wagon.
We're in a covered wagon.
We're in a covered wagon,
A-bumpin' down the trail!

We're in a covered wagon.
We're in a covered wagon.
We're in a covered wagon,
A-rockin' down the trail!

After singing the song a few times, direct the wagon drivers to form a circle with their wagons. At the end of the day, encourage your youngsters to take their wagons home and share the wagon train story with their families.

Workers Of The West

The Spring Roundup

Cowboys were essential to the Old West's cattle industry. A very important duty of the cowboy was to take part in the roundups every spring and fall. During a roundup, cowboys from several different ranches would work together and drive all the cattle in the open range to a central location. There they would read the brands on the cattle and sort them according to their markings. Any new calves would be branded with their mothers' markings.

Give your little cowhands a roundup experience. Duplicate the cow patterns on page 73 several times on manila paper. Color the cow pictures and cut them out; then label each cow with one of three different brands, such as shapes or letters. Make an index-card label for each of the three brands and affix each label to a berry-basket corral. Have student volunteers sort the cattle into the correct corrals. Encourage the rest of the group to give the cowhands a low, "Moo!" for a job well done!

Strike It Rich!

Thousands of people flocked to the West in search of gold and silver—but only a fraction of those people were lucky enough to find it. Even so, the deposits that were discovered were numerous enough and large enough that mining became a popular vocation in the West.

Send your little prospectors off to seek their fortunes with this precious-metal search. Label eight large index cards with numerals, letters, or colors, and insert them in a pocket chart. Have your students close their eyes while you place a piece of candy wrapped in silver or gold foil behind one card. Invite a student volunteer to name a card. Lift that card to see if she found the gold or silver. If not, keep the card and continue with another volunteer. Once the gold or silver is found, re-place the cards and keep students digging until they're all rich—with chocolate!

Express Delivery

The fastest way to send mail in the Old West was through the pony express. Approximately 80 riders rode about 400 fast horses in order to get mail cross-country in 10 days or less. The pony express ran day and night—in all kinds of weather.

Take your class outside and divide them into small, equal groups. Position each member of one group at a different station between two designated points. Give the first child in that group a letter and use a stopwatch to time how long it takes for the letter to reach its destination. Have each group take a turn; then compare the groups' times.

Western Wildlife

Critter Booklets

Introduce your little pioneers to critters of the Old West with this booklet idea. Duplicate the wildlife patterns on page 73 and the booklet cover on page 74 for each child. Then make one extra copy of the cover without the title and illustration details. Print the booklet text (as shown) on this blank copy. Then make five copies of this text page for each child.

Have the child color and cut out his cover. Then have him color the five wildlife pictures, cut them out, and glue one picture on each programmed booklet page. Assist him with writing the name of the appropriate critter in the blank on each page. Direct the child to cut out all the booklet pages and assemble them behind his cover. Staple the pages and cover together along the left edge. Challenge students to take their booklets home and ask their families to help find out one interesting fact about one of these animals. When the booklets are returned to school, let the children share their newfound knowledge with the class.

Way Out West

After discussing the critters of the West, teach your youngsters to sing this song to the tune of "Old MacDonald."

Way out West are [buffaloes]. Yippie-yippie-oh!
Way out West are [buffaloes]. Yippie-yippie-oh!
With a [stomp, stomp] here and a [stomp, stomp] there.
Here a [stomp], there a [stomp], everywhere a
  [stomp, stomp].
Way out West are [buffaloes]. Yippie-yippie-oh!

Way out West are [prairie dogs]. Yippie-yippie-oh!
Way out West are [prairie dogs]. Yippie-yippie-oh!
With a [bark, bark] here and a [bark, bark] there.
Here a [bark], there a [bark], everywhere a [bark, bark].
Way out West are [prairie dogs]. Yippie-yippie-oh!

Repeat the song, substituting the names and sounds of other Western critters:
  rattlesnakes—hiss, hiss—hiss
  jackrabbits—twitch, twitch—twitch
  coyotes—howl, howl—howl

Wild West Critters

Out in the West, there will be a <u>rattlesnake</u> for me to see.

69

Readiness Rodeo

Your little rustlers will stampede to these activity centers to show off their readiness skills.

Baffling Boots

Give your students problem-solving practice with these boot puzzles. Enlarge one of the boot cards on page 75; then make four copies of the enlarged boot. Decorate these boots with bright-colored markers, making sure they are distinctly different from one another. Laminate them if desired; then cut each boot into four pieces. Store each boot puzzle in a resealable plastic bag, or—for more advanced children—mix all of the boot pieces together in a shoebox to be sorted before solving the puzzles.

Cactus Counting

Use the booklet cover pattern on page 74 to make these cute counting cards. Mask the title and the illustrations of the spines; then reproduce the pattern on green paper. Place a different numeral sticker on the small cactus arm on the right side of each pattern. Provide two-inch pieces of brown pipe cleaner to represent the cactuses' spines. Have youngsters count and place the correct number of spines on each corresponding cactus card.

Boot Buddies

Reproduce the boot cards on page 75 on construction paper to make a high-kickin' Concentration game. Copy enough of the cards to make as many pairs of boots as are appropriate for your group. Cut apart the cards and color each pair of boots identically. Laminate the cutouts if desired. Your little buckaroos will love this challenging visual-discrimination activity.

Cactus Collages

Let each youngster create a large collage of a cactus using a mixed-media technique. The collage should be completed in the following four steps:

Step 1: Paint a strip of glue at the bottom of the page; then sprinkle sand onto the glue.

Step 2: Use colored chalk to draw and color a cactus base.

Step 3: Sponge-paint several cactus arms that touch the base.

Step 4: Glue toothpick spines to the cactus collage.

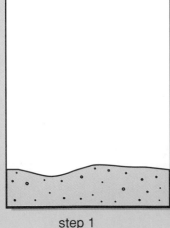

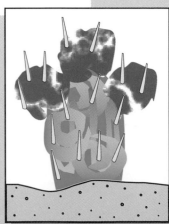

| step 1 | step 2 | step 3 | step 4 |

Cowboy Lullaby

Teach your youngsters this easy action poem, and they'll really feel like Wild West wranglers!

Way out West   *(Point straight ahead.)*
Where the stars are bright,   *(Hold hand above eyes like a sun visor.)*
I sing a song   *(Pretend to strum a guitar.)*
By the campfire light.   *(Hold hands outstretched as if warming them in front of a fire.)*

I ride my horse   *(Pretend to ride a horse.)*
On the wide prairie.   *(Stretch arms out wide.)*
We gallop along—   *("Gallop" hands on thighs.)*
My pony and me.   *(Pretend to pet a horse.)*

I watch ten cows   *(Hold up ten fingers.)*
That snort and moo.   *(Snort and moo!)*
I sing them to sleep   *(Pretend to strum a guitar.)*
When the day is through. *(Close eyes and pretend to sleep.)*

Books For The Bunkhouse

Nell Nugget And The Cow Caper
Written by Judith Ross Enderle and
   Stephanie Gordon Tessler
Published by Simon & Schuster Books
   For Young Readers

White Dynamite And Curly Kidd
Written by Bill Martin Jr. and
   John Archambault
Published by Holt, Rinehart and Winston

Someday Rider
Written by Ann Herbert Scott
Published by Clarion Books

Sam's Wild West Show
Written by Nancy Antle
Published by Dial Books For Young
   Readers

We Made It!

Back on the home front safe and sound! Treat your little ones to a special souvenir from the Wild West—a sheriff's badge. Reproduce the star and circle patterns from page 72 onto tagboard for each child. Have the child cut out these shapes, assisting her as necessary. Direct her to apply a layer of glue to the circle and sprinkle gold glitter to cover the glue. Then ask her to paint the star cutout with gray or silver tempera paint. When both pieces are dry, help her write her name on the star with a black marker; then glue the star on top of the circle. Hot-glue a pin fastener to the back of the circle and pin the badge to the child's clothing. Never fear— the deputies are here!

Hat And Badge Patterns

Use the hat pattern with "Headband Hats" on page 66.
Use the circle and star with "We Made It!" on page 71.

Place on fold of file folder.

©1996 The Education Center, Inc. • *MAY* • TEC249

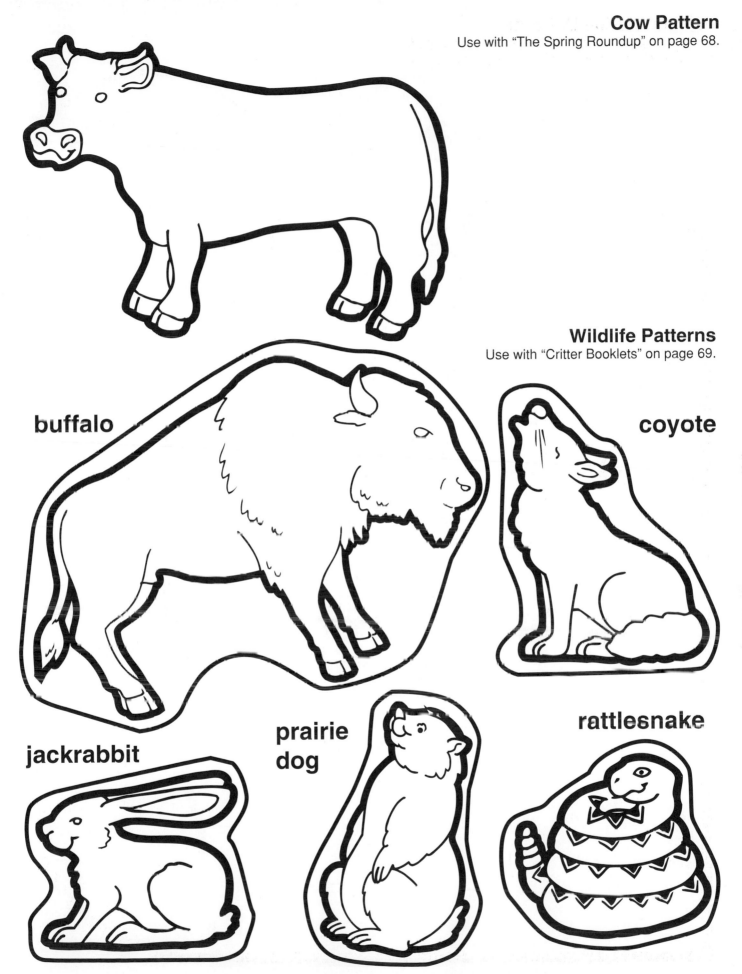

Cow Pattern
Use with "The Spring Roundup" on page 68.

Wildlife Patterns
Use with "Critter Booklets" on page 69.

buffalo

coyote

jackrabbit

prairie dog

rattlesnake

Booklet Cover

Use with "Critter Booklets" on page 69 and "Cactus Counting" on page 70.

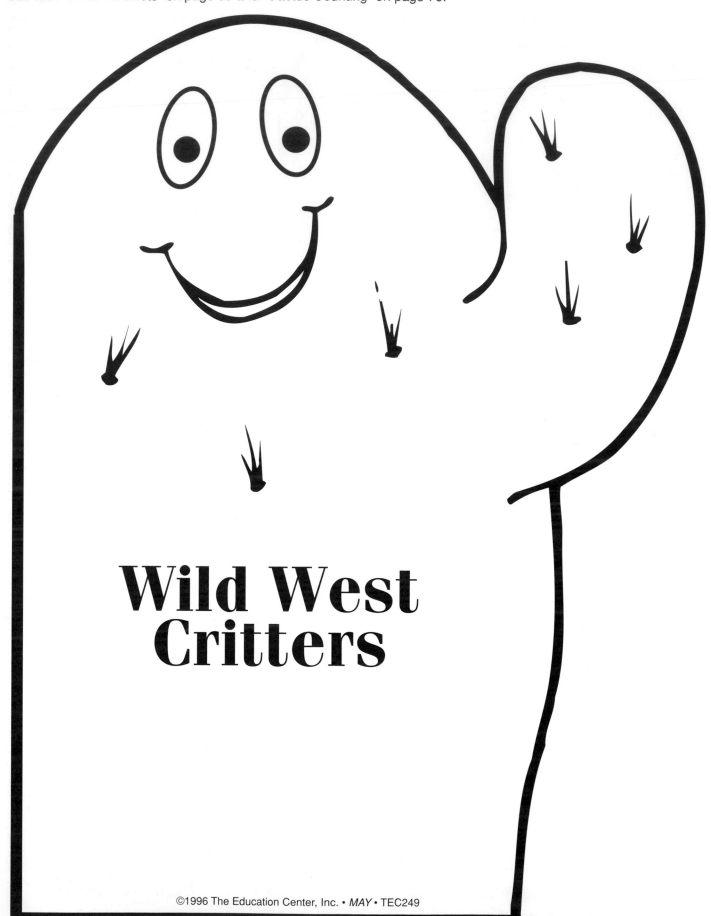

Wild West Critters

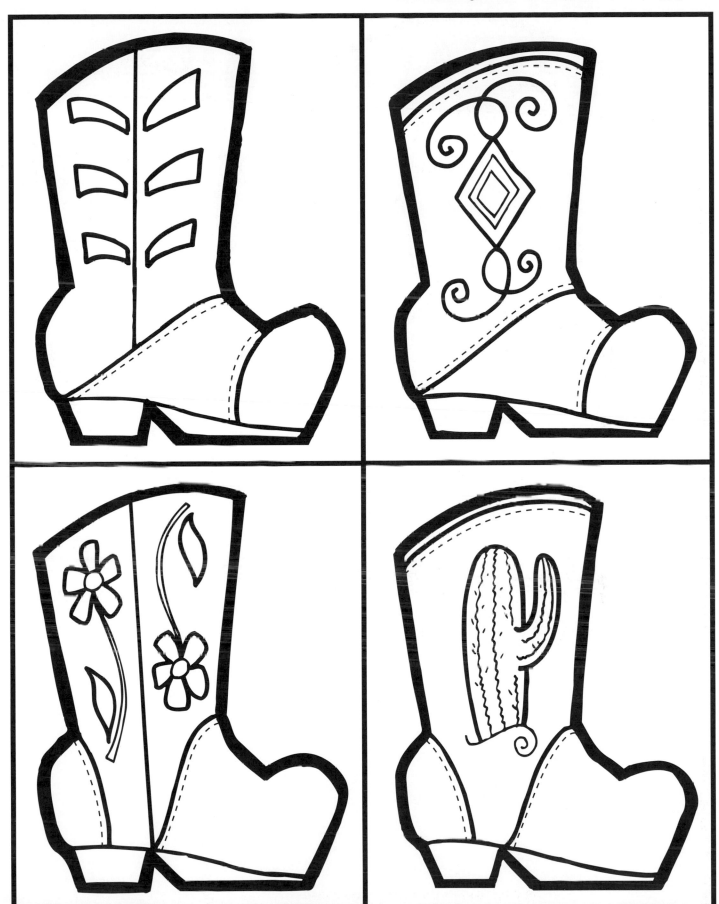

Red Berries...Ripe Berries...
STRAWBERRIES

Use some of these ready-to-pick strawberry ideas to provide opportunities for youngsters to ripen their language arts, science, math, social, and motor skills.

ideas contributed by Catherine Dane-McDougal, Debbie Jerrett and Mackie Rhodes

Strawberries In The Spotlight

Call attention to this delightful and delicious fruit known as a strawberry by placing it in the spotlight. In advance send home a note with each child requesting his parents to donate a small basket of strawberries to the class. (The strawberries will be used in various activities throughout this unit.) During group time, give each child a washed strawberry to examine—to look at, feel, smell, and even taste. Then invite each child in turn to describe one thing about his fruit as you shine a flashlight on his strawberry. Write each child's observation on a large, strawberry-shaped cutout. Display the cutout in the center described in "Keeping 'Berry' Busy" on page 78.

How Does Your Strawberry Field Grow?

Youngsters will be fascinated to discover the extensive growth of strawberry plants when they take a trip to a strawberry patch. Prior to visiting the patch, explain that strawberry plants—like all plants—need sun and water in order to grow. Tell students that the plant grows three-leaflet clusters along its long stems—called *runners.* Small white flowers bloom on the plant, then wither, as a greenish-white strawberry appears and grows from the green *cap* left on the flower stalk. Then the seed-covered strawberry ripens to a bright red and is ready to be picked.

While at the patch, obtain permission for youngsters to carefully examine the parts of a strawberry plant and to pick a few ripe strawberries to take back to your classroom. Engage students in a lively rendition of this song as they participate in strawberry picking. If a visit to a strawberry field is not possible, bring a strawberry plant and some fresh strawberries to class for students to examine.

The Strawberry Patch
(sung to the tune of "The Paw Paw Patch")

Pickin' up strawberries.
Puttin' 'em in the basket.
Pickin' up strawberries.
Puttin' 'em in the basket.
Pickin' up strawberries.
Puttin' 'em in the basket.
Way down yonder in the strawberry patch!

strawberries are red.
Lisa
They have black dots.
Jeffrey
They taste sweet.
Amber

Strawberry Pull-Through Story

Reinforce the needs and growth of a strawberry plant with this simple prop and rhyme. Make five or six of these props and have small groups take turns using them. First duplicate the story-rhyme patterns on page 82 on tagboard. Color and cut out each pattern; then laminate them for durability. Color the bottom side of a paper-plate half to resemble a strawberry. Knot one end of a two-foot length of green ribbon. Fold the plate's straight edge to form a cone, trapping the knotted end of the ribbon just below the point of the cone. Staple the ribbon and cone point in place; then staple the straight edges together to create a strawberry shape. Glue a green construction-paper cap along the strawberry top. Then attach the strawberry cutout to the ribbon so that it is visible just above the strawberry cap when the ribbon is pulled taut. Attach the flower, raindrop, and sun cutouts—in that order—at even intervals along the remainder of the ribbon, leaving the end free. To use the prop, tuck the cutouts into the top of the strawberry. Gently pull the end of the ribbon to reveal each cutout as it is mentioned in this rhyme. If desired, glue a copy of the rhyme to the front of the strawberry.

> Strawberry, Strawberry, how do you grow?
> With sun and water, don't you know.
> First blooms a flower that smells so sweet.
> Then grows a strawberry—a tasty treat!

A Sweet Surprise

Invite youngsters to map out the development of a strawberry plant in these individual booklets. For each child, duplicate pages 83–85 on white construction paper. Have each child cut apart his booklet cover and pages, then glue pages 1–4 together as indicated. Instruct him to complete the booklet pages following the provided suggestions; then have him glue the cover and last page to the booklet as indicated. After he accordion-folds his booklet, encourage the child to take it home to share with his family.

- **Cover:** Color the ground along the bottom of the page. Write your name on the line.
- **Pages 1–4:** Color the ground. Glue a length of green yarn along the strawberry vine. Glue a green construction-paper leaf cutout on each X.
- **Page 3:** Sponge-paint a red circle at the end of each short stem. Twist the middle of a small square of green tissue paper; then glue it on top of each red circle.
- **Page 4–5:** Sponge-paint a red heart at the end of the vine on page 4; then sponge-paint a few hearts on page 5. Glue a twisted square of green tissue paper on the top of each heart. If desired, dot each strawberry with a black marker to create seeds.

A Sweet Surprise

by Stephen Doughty

Strawberries!

Keeping "Berry" Busy

Provide youngsters with the opportunity to practice a variety of skills in this strawberry learning center. To prepare, place several containers of strawberries, several empty containers of different sizes, strawberry baskets, sticky notes, pencils, a scale, a few small objects, and a ruler in the center. Or, if you prefer not to use real strawberries, have each student make a few play-dough strawberries. To make a strawberry, instruct the child to form a small ball of red play dough into a strawberry shape, then cap it with a sculpted piece of green play dough. Have him poke rice onto the surface of the strawberry to represent the seeds. Then invite student pairs to engage in some of the following activities:

- Estimate the number of strawberries in each container of a different size. Write the estimation on a sticky note and attach it to the container; then count the strawberries in each container. Compare the estimation to the actual number of strawberries.

- Organize a set of strawberries into a pattern—such as by size or orientation (for example: *cap to the left, cap to the right*).

- Put the corresponding number of strawberries into each of several strawberry baskets labeled with different numerals.

- Place a small object on one side of a balance scale; then balance the scale using strawberries. Count the number of strawberries used to achieve balance.

- Measure the length of an object using strawberries. Count the number of strawberries. Then use a ruler to measure the actual length of the object.

Strawberry Squish Paint

Youngsters are bound to squeeze some fun out of making this unique paint! To make strawberry squish paint, give each child three strawberries. Have him put his fruit in a resealable plastic sandwich bag; then help him gently press out the air as he securely seals the bag. Invite the child to hand-mash—or squish—the strawberries in the bag until a liquidlike consistency is achieved. Then provide each child with a sheet of white construction paper and a paintbrush. Encourage him to paint designs, letters, or numbers on his paper using the squish paint. If he desires, allow the child to finger-paint with the fruit paint also. After the paintings dry, display them with the title "Strawberry Creations."

I Am A Strawberry

You'll find yourself in the midst of a human strawberry patch when students use these strawberry masks as they sing this little ditty. In advance cut a class supply of paper plates into strawberry shapes. To make a mask, have each child paint a strawberry plate red. After the paint dries, have him use a marker to draw seeds onto the strawberry plate. Help him cut an eye window; then instruct him to glue tufts of green tissue paper or cellophane along the top edge of the strawberry to represent the cap. Attach a wide craft stick to the bottom of the strawberry. Then teach youngsters this song. Invite them to hold their masks in front of their faces as they sing.

(sung to the tune of "I'm A Little Teapot")

I am a strawberry,
Red and sweet.
See all my seeds
And my cap so neat.

When I grow ripe
And ready to eat,
Pop off my cap—
A tasty treat!

Strawberry Countdown

It's picking time! That's the opinion of the mouse in this fingerplay! Engage youngsters in some countdown role-playing as they participate in saying this rhyme. To prepare, duplicate the fingerplay patterns on page 82 on tagboard; then cut out each pattern to use as a template for the fingerplay figures. Cut out five red felt strawberries and five green felt caps. Cut the slits as indicated on each cap. Dot seeds onto each of the strawberries with a black permanent marker. Form, then hot-glue, the strawberry into a cone shape; then hot-glue each strawberry onto a separate cap as shown. Hot-glue wiggle eyes, a pom-pom nose, yarn whiskers, and felt ears onto the toe end of a sock to resemble a mouse. Invite each child in turn to place a strawberry on each finger of one hand and to wear the mouse puppet on her other hand. Recite the rhyme, replacing the underlined number with *four, three, two,* and *one,* consecutively, for each repetition of the rhyme. Each time the rhyme indicates, have the child remove a strawberry from a finger with the mouse puppet.

[Five] little strawberries growing on a vine,
Turning juicy red in the bright sunshine.
Along came a mouse and picked one sweet,
Then nibbled on a scrumptious strawberry treat.

An Inspired Flavor

Help little ones become familiar with some of the many foods inspired by the flavor of strawberries. Ask youngsters to name as many different foods as possible that are made with strawberries or have a strawberry flavor—such as ice cream, jelly, toaster pastries, yogurt, gelatin, and powdered drink mix. Write their responses on a sheet of chart paper. Then arrange separate sampling stations for several different strawberry-flavored foods. For each station prepare a small, individual sample of that food for each child. Place a marker and a large strawberry cutout labeled with a "Yes" and a "No" column at each station. Give each child a large, ripe strawberry on a napkin; then invite him to taste a sample of the food in each station. After tasting each food, encourage him to take a small bite of his strawberry, then decide if he prefers the real strawberry to the flavored food. Have him write his name under the appropriate column on the cutout to indicate his preference. After the taste sampling has been completed, review the results with students.

Strawberry Sippers

Whether they prefer the flavor of real strawberries or not, this simple recipe will have youngsters sipping up a streak of strawberry slush. Help each child prepare his serving individually or have several youngsters combine their ingredients together. Pour the resulting treats into cups, add straws, and watch your little ones enter a world of sipping pleasure.

Strawberry Sipper For One

5 medium or large strawberries, stems and caps removed
1/2 cup milk or ice cream

Put the ingredients in a blender. Place the lid on the blender; then puree the mixture.

Upside-Down Strawberry Delight

Here's another scrumptious strawberry treat for little ones to create and then to eat! Add green food coloring to a container of whipped topping. Have each child use a plastic knife to spread some whipped topping on a vanilla wafer, then top her cookie with an upside-down strawberry (with the cap removed). Invite each child to enjoy her tasty creation.

Strawberry Stories To Share

Pass around a basket of strawberries for youngsters to nibble on as they enjoy these strawberry stories.

The big, hungry bear ate six strawberries.

The Little Mouse, The Red Ripe Strawberry, And The Big Hungry Bear

By Don and Audrey Wood
Published by Child's Play

After reading this story aloud, invite youngsters to make a class big book about the big, hungry bear. Ask each child to draw a picture of what he imagines the big, hungry bear to look like. Then have him cut out his picture and glue it to a large sheet of construction paper. Sequence the students' drawings by size; then glue paper strips programmed with "The big, hungry bear ate [one] strawberry" on each child's page except the last—the page with the largest bear. Program that page with "The big, hungry bear was FULL!" Then fill in a numeral on each text strip according to the position of that picture in the sequence—"one" for the first picture, "two" for the second, and so on—assigning a different number to each page. Bind the pages between two construction-paper covers and write the title "The Big, Hungry Bear" on the front. Invite each child to draw the indicated number of strawberries on his page. Place the book in the reading center for youngsters to enjoy.

The Grey Lady And The Strawberry Snatcher

By Molly Bang
Published by Simon & Schuster Books For Young Readers

Share this wordless book with students; then engage them in a game that is sure to snatch their attention. Invite a student volunteer to role-play the grey lady (you might have her don a grey cape—a fabric length or towel fastened around her shoulders). Have her sit in a chair with her back to the group. Place a felt strawberry or red beanbag under her chair. Have the other students sit with their hands hidden behind their backs. In a whisper, instruct one child—the strawberry snatcher—to sneak up and snatch the strawberry, then return to his seat, hiding the strawberry behind his back. Then have the class say "Grey Lady, Grey Lady, who snatched your strawberry?" The grey lady turns to face the class and to identify the strawberry snatcher. Provide clues—such as clothing or hair color—to help the grey lady correctly name the culprit. Then have the strawberry snatcher and the grey lady switch positions and repeat the game, this time selecting a different child to be the strawberry snatcher. Continue the game until every child has had the opportunity to role-play the grey lady or the strawberry snatcher.

Story-Rhyme Patterns
Use with "Strawberry Pull-Through Story" on page 77.

sun

raindrop

flower

strawberry

Fingerplay Patterns
Use with "Strawberry Countdown" on page 79.

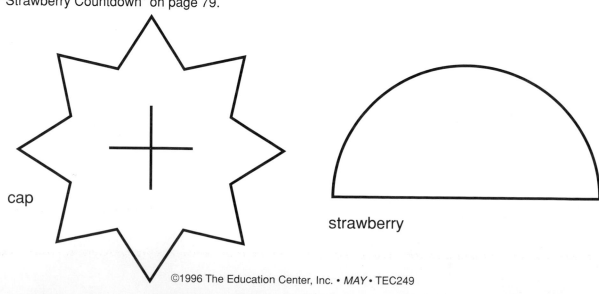

cap

strawberry

A Sweet Surprise

by _____

Glue page 1 here.

What grows on a vine so wild and free?

1

Glue page 2 here.

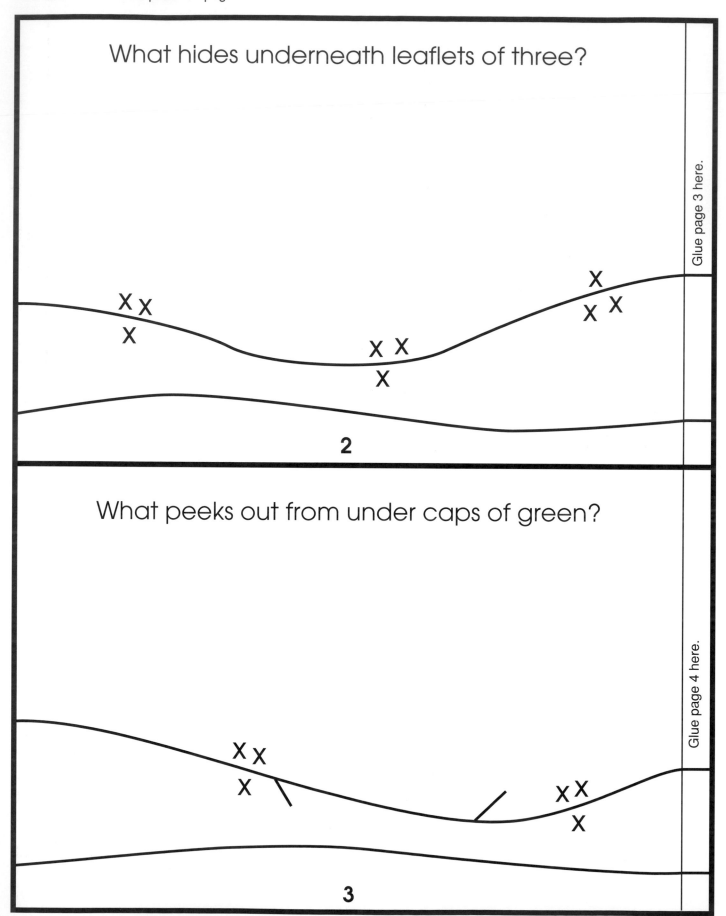

What hides underneath leaflets of three?

2

What peeks out from under caps of green?

3

The tastiest fruit you've ever seen...

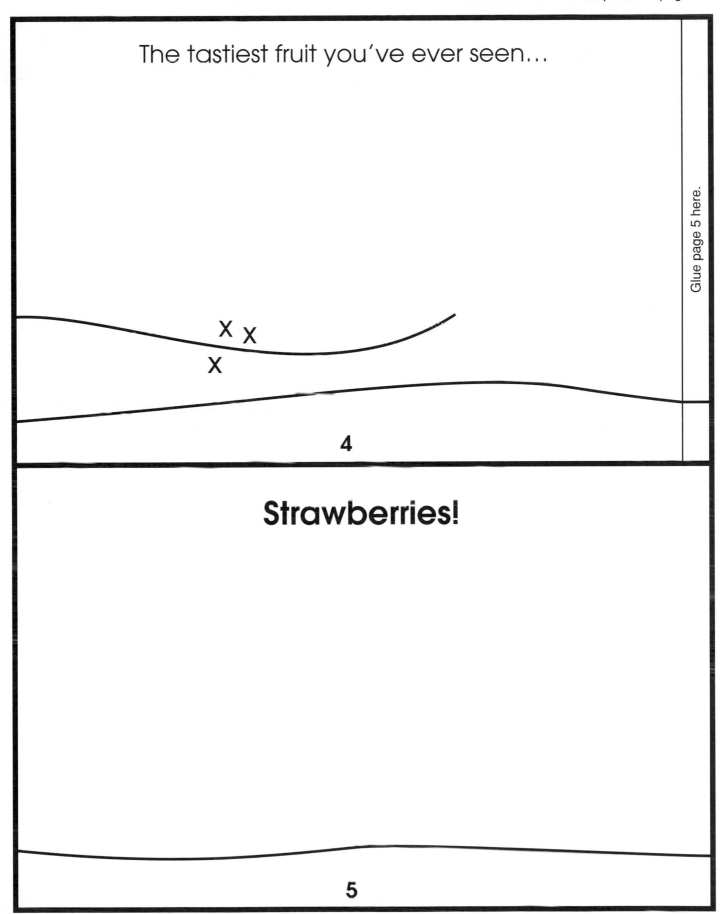

Glue page 5 here.

4

Strawberries!

5

A Day At The Beach

Generate a wave of learning excitement when you and
your youngsters use this cross-curricular beach unit!

ideas contributed by Barbara Backer and Mackie Rhodes

Sand, Surf, And Sun

Dive into your beach study by reading aloud
At The Beach by Anne and Harlow Rockwell
(Macmillan Publishing Company). Afterward find
out if any students have ever been to the beach.
Ask them to tell about their experiences—the
things they did or saw at the beach. Encourage
those students who have not been to the beach
to tell about an imaginary beach experience.
Randomly write their responses on a length of
light brown butcher paper edged along the bottom with a blue paper-strip wave. If desired,
place a sticky note labeled with each child's
name beside her response. Invite several children at a time to find their responses, then illustrate and autograph them. Remove all the sticky
notes from the completed beach scene; then
display the scene with the title "At The Beach."

Packing Up

A trip to the beach means planning ahead and
packing necessary items to make it a fun day in
the sun. Engage youngsters in some critical de-
cision-making and organizational skills by having
them pack a bag for a beach adventure. To prepare, gather a large beach bag and an assortment of items that may be used at the beach—
such as sunglasses, sunscreen, a beach towel,
a swimsuit, a pail, and a shovel. Add some other
unrelated objects to the collection, also—such as
blocks, a flashlight, and a coat. Invite each student in turn to select an appropriate item from
the collection to take to the beach. Ask him to
explain why he made his choice; then have him
put the item in the bag. After the bag is packed
and ready to go, put it aside to use with "The
Beach At Last!" on page 87.

In The Shade

The beach forecast calls for bright sunshine—but the sun's glare will
be no problem for youngsters when they make these sun visors to wear!
To prepare, duplicate the sun-visor pattern on page 92 on tagboard for
each child. Have the child cut out the pattern, then decorate it with sea-
creature sponge prints. To make a visor band, cut out the center of a paper plate. Keep the center cutout for use in "Cool Breezes" on page 87.
Cut through the resulting outer ring; then round the ends to resemble a
sun visor. Have each child glue his visor cutout along the edge of the
band. Then place the visors aside for youngsters to wear during the
imaginary beach trip in "The Beach At Last!" on page 87.

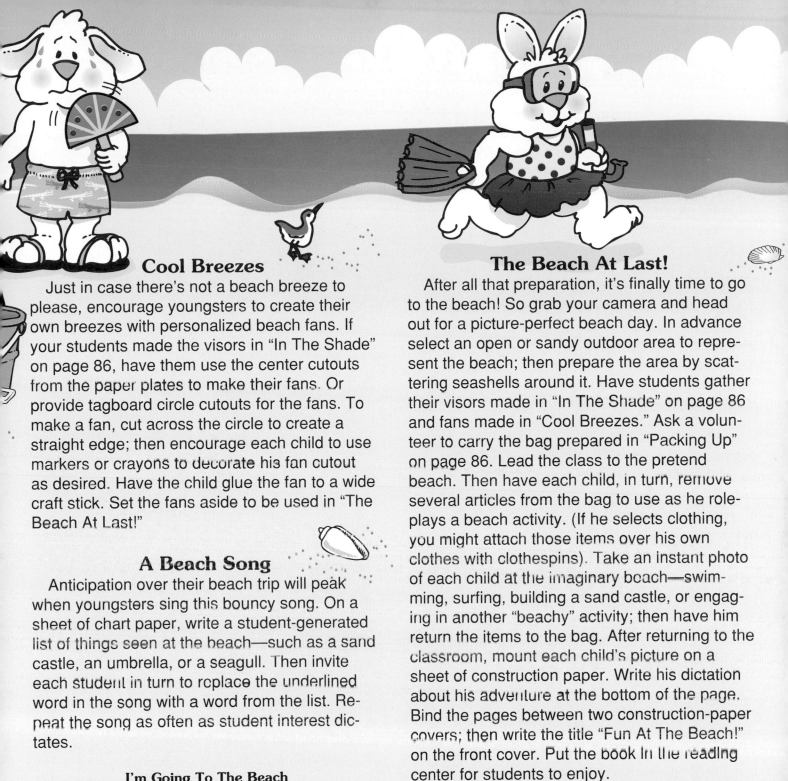

Cool Breezes

Just in case there's not a beach breeze to please, encourage youngsters to create their own breezes with personalized beach fans. If your students made the visors in "In The Shade" on page 86, have them use the center cutouts from the paper plates to make their fans. Or provide tagboard circle cutouts for the fans. To make a fan, cut across the circle to create a straight edge; then encourage each child to use markers or crayons to decorate his fan cutout as desired. Have the child glue the fan to a wide craft stick. Set the fans aside to be used in "The Beach At Last!"

A Beach Song

Anticipation over their beach trip will peak when youngsters sing this bouncy song. On a sheet of chart paper, write a student-generated list of things seen at the beach—such as a sand castle, an umbrella, or a seagull. Then invite each student in turn to replace the underlined word in the song with a word from the list. Repeat the song as often as student interest dictates.

I'm Going To The Beach
(sung to the tune of "The Farmer In The Dell")

I'm going to the beach.
I'm going to the beach.
I think I'll see a [lifeguard] there.
I'm going to the beach!

The Beach At Last!

After all that preparation, it's finally time to go to the beach! So grab your camera and head out for a picture-perfect beach day. In advance select an open or sandy outdoor area to represent the beach; then prepare the area by scattering seashells around it. Have students gather their visors made in "In The Shade" on page 86 and fans made in "Cool Breezes." Ask a volunteer to carry the bag prepared in "Packing Up" on page 86. Lead the class to the pretend beach. Then have each child, in turn, remove several articles from the bag to use as he role-plays a beach activity. (If he selects clothing, you might attach those items over his own clothes with clothespins). Take an instant photo of each child at the imaginary beach—swimming, surfing, building a sand castle, or engaging in another "beachy" activity; then have him return the items to the bag. After returning to the classroom, mount each child's picture on a sheet of construction paper. Write his dictation about his adventure at the bottom of the page. Bind the pages between two construction-paper covers; then write the title "Fun At The Beach!" on the front cover. Put the book in the reading center for students to enjoy.

Extend this imaginary beach experience for youngsters by preparing the activities described on pages 88 and 89 in advance. If desired take photos of students participating in all the additional activities, and add them to the class book.

Baking At The Beach

Youngsters will be cooking up some creative sand recipes of their own after being introduced to Papa Bear's method of cake making in *Sand Cake* by Frank Asch (Putnam Publishing Group). Prior to reading the story, partially fill a plastic swimming pool, or several dishpans, with sand. Place a plastic shovel and pail, a variety of sand molds, a water-filled spray bottle, and a few natural items—such as sticks, feathers, and leaves—near each sand container. (If you plan to include this activity with "The Beach At Last!" on page 87, you might pack the book in the beach bag; then remove it when you are ready to read it.) Read the book aloud to youngsters; then invite pairs of students to use the provided materials to create sand pictures and lots of imaginary recipes and characters. Encourage each child to tell his partner about his creations.

Bare Feet

The sandy surface of the beach provides a truly "sense-sational" barefoot experience. Invite youngsters to take off their socks and shoes, and give their soles the feel of the beach—as well as a variety of other surfaces—with this activity. In advance duplicate a class supply of the starfish pattern on page 96 on construction paper. Then prepare a container of sand as described in "Baking At The Beach." Place the sand container beside a sidewalk, if possible; then place several large pieces of materials with different textures—such as plastic bubble wrap, a carpet square, a straw mat, and a carpet of Bristle Blocks®—beside the container. Have each child cut out her starfish pattern and write her name on it. Then invite each child in turn to walk barefoot in the sand, on the sidewalk, and on each type of material. Encourage her to describe the feel of each texture—soft, rough, scratchy, or hard. Then have her put her cutout next to the texture on which she most enjoyed walking. After every student has had a turn, have the class count the number of starfish beside each texture and determine which surface is the class favorite.

Sand Stepping

While youngsters have their shoes off, invite them to make some sand footprints. Prepare a tray of tempera paint mixed with sand and dishwashing liquid. Place the paint at one end of a length of bulletin-board paper; then place a dishpan of water and an old towel at the other end of the paper. Have each student in a small group, in turn, step barefoot into the tray of paint, then walk across the paper. Have him rinse his feet in the water, then air- or towel-dry them. Label each child's footprints with his name. Paint glue on the areas of the paper surrounding the footprints; then sprinkle sand over the glue. Repeat the process with each small group of students using a different length of paper each time. When the paint and glue have dried, display the sandy footprints with the title "Sand Stepping." As youngsters view the display, encourage each child to count his footprints and compare the size of his prints with those of his classmates.

If The Shell Fits...

Move into it! Fascinate little ones with facts about the hermit crab's transient lifestyle; then invite them to explore size relationships in this discovery center. To prepare, collect several hard blocks—wooden or plastic—of different sizes and shapes. Cut a sponge to match the size and dimension of each hard block. Then gather an assortment of boxes in various sizes and shapes. Tell youngsters that a hermit crab lives inside a shell in order to protect its soft body. To get inside the shell, the crab twists and curls its body. When it grows too big for its shell, the crab moves into a larger one.

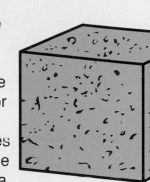

Invite each child in turn to compare the sizes, shapes, and textures of the blocks in the center. Then ask her to pretend that each sponge block is a soft-bodied hermit crab searching for a new shell home—a box. Instruct her to fit each make-believe crab into a shell. Have her place the corresponding hard block beside each box containing a sponge crab. Prompt her to compare each block to the box. Will the hard block fit inside the box? Why or why not? Why did the corresponding sponge block fit in the box? If the hard block were a crab, would it need a shell? Why or why not? Then encourage the child to engage in some dramatic beach play using the blocks and boxes as well as other props to represent beach life.

House Hunting

Teach youngsters this rhyme and the corresponding hand gestures about a house-hunting hermit crab.

Hermit crab has a special house.	*Form roof with hands.*
He lives in a borrowed shell.	*Cup one hand over other fist.*
But when he grows much bigger,	*Spread open hands apart.*
The shell doesn't fit so well.	*Shake head from side to side.*
Up and down the beach he goes,	*Point finger back and forth.*
Scanning left and right.	*Point finger left and right.*
Searching for a brand-new house—	*Shade eyes with hand.*
A shell that fits just right.	*Cup one hand over other fist.*
When he finds that perfect shell,	*Point finger at pretend shell.*
You see him almost grin.	*Point to mouth and smile.*
"Hello, new house!" he seems to say,	*Wave at pretend shell.*
"I think I'll move right in!"	*Slide fist into cupped hand.*

89

I Went To The Beach

Youngsters will enjoy learning new hand signs as they recite this verse about a visit to the beach. If desired, encourage students to create additional verses and hand signs to add to these.

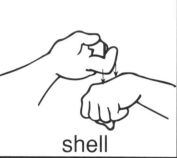
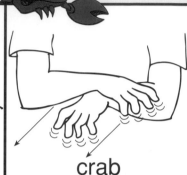

I went to the beach
And what did I see?
A *bird* on the sand
Looking at me!

I went to the beach
And what did I see?
A *fish* in the water
Splashing at me!

I went to the beach
And what did I see?
A *shell* in the sand
Sparkling at me!

I went to the beach
And what did I see?
A *crab* in its shell
Waving at me!

bird   fish   shell   crab

Beach Booklets

Students will be delighted to share the rhyme in "I Went To The Beach" with their families using these individual booklets. For each child, duplicate the booklet pages on page 93 on white construction paper; then make two construction-paper copies of the shell pattern on page 96 for each child. Have the child cut apart the booklet pages and shell patterns, then stack the pages between the shell booklet covers. Staple the booklet along the left edge and write the title "I Went To The Beach" on the front cover. Instruct youngsters to complete each page following the suggestions provided; then invite them to take their booklets home to read with their families.

- Page 1: Trace the bird footprints with glue; then sprinkle sand over the glue.
- Page 2: Sponge-print a fish on the page. After the paint dries, glue a wiggle eye onto the fish.
- Page 3: Color the shell with glitter crayons.
- Page 4: Use watercolors and a cotton swab to paint the crab.

Beach Reading

A Beach Day
Written by Douglas Florian
Published by Greenwillow Books

A House For Hermit Crab
Written by Eric Carle
Published by Picture Book Studio

One Sun: A Book Of Terse Verse
Written by Bruce McMillan
Published by Scholastic Inc.

Sea Squares
Written by Joy N. Hulme
Published by Hyperion Books For Children

Beach Games To Go

Prepare these games for youngsters to use during their beach study, or at any time of the year. Simply duplicate a supply of the game pictures on page 94; then prepare each game following the provided suggestions. Store each set of game cards in a separate resealable plastic bag labeled with the name of the game.

- **Beach Memory**
  Duplicate ten sets of the shell patterns on page 96 on construction paper. Cut out each set of shell cards; then glue one duplicated picture from page 94 onto the back of each shell card, to make ten matching pairs. Laminate the cards for durability. Spread the cards facedown on the floor or table. To use, have each player turn over two cards. If the cards match, the student keeps them. If the cards do not match, have the child return the cards facedown. Continue play with the next child, until all the matches have been found.

- **Beach Dominoes**
  Have each youngster cut apart one sheet of game pictures. Instruct him to glue each picture onto a separate end of a divided notecard to create a domino. Stack the completed dominoes together. Place one domino faceup; then give six dominoes to each player in a small group of students. Invite each player in turn to place the end of one of her dominoes next to the matching end of a domino on the playing surface. If she does not have a matching domino, invite her to draw a domino from the stack. Continue the game until no additional matches can be made.

- **Beach Bingo**
  Duplicate and cut out six sets of the shell patterns on page 96 on construction paper. Also duplicate the bingo card on page 95 on construction paper for each child. Have him cut out his card; then have him cut out and glue eight different game pictures onto his card. Create caller cards by gluing each different game picture onto a separate shell card. If desired, laminate the caller cards for durability. To play, provide each player with a supply of small sea shells to use as markers. Have a volunteer randomly pull a caller card from a box, then name the picture on the card. If that picture is on a player's card, he may cover it with a marker. After a player has marked every picture on his card, he calls out "Beach Bingo!" Continue play until each player has covered all the pictures on his card.

- **Go Shell Hunting**
  To prepare for this modified Go Fish game, make four sets of cards as described in "Beach Memory" (for a total of 40 cards). To play, pass four cards to each player in a small group of students; then place the deck of cards facedown on the table. Have each player in turn ask the child to his right for a specific card that matches a card he is holding. If the child has that card, he gives it to the first player, who then places the match on the table. If the child does not have the card, he tells the first player to "Go shell hunting." The first player takes the top card off the deck and keeps that card in his hand unless it matches one of his cards. Continue play in this manner until all the matches have been made.

Sun-Visor Pattern
Use with "In The Shade" on page 86.

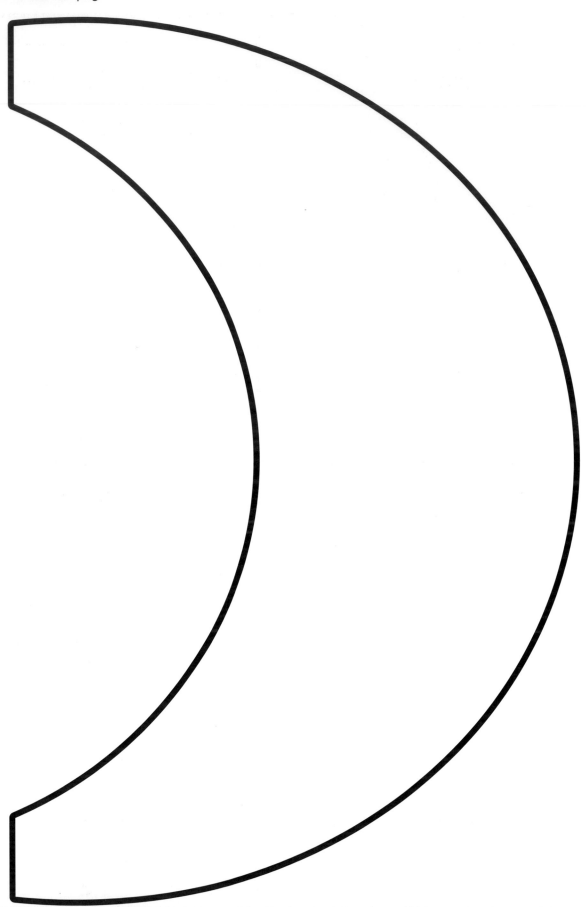

I went to the beach
And what did I see?

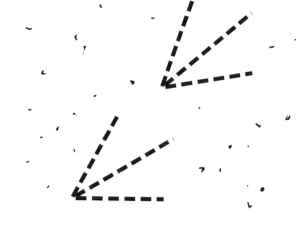

A *bird* on the sand
Looking at me!

1

I went to the beach
And what did I see?

A *fish* in the water
Splashing at me!

2

I went to the beach
And what did I see?

A *shell* in the sand
Sparkling at me!

3

I went to the beach
And what did I see?

A *crab* in its shell
Waving at me!

4

Game Picture Cards
Use with "Beach Games To Go" on page 91.

Beach Bingo

Starfish Patterns
Use with "Bare Feet" on page 88.

Shell Patterns
Use with "Beach Booklets" on page 90 and "Beach Games To Go" on page 91.

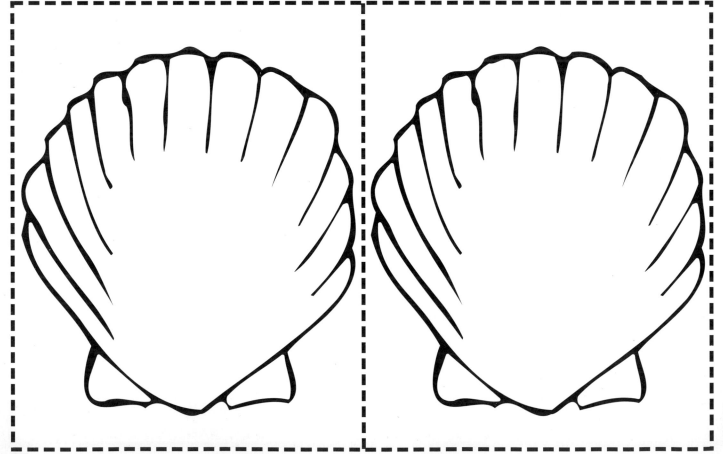